Windows XP
Pocket Reference

Windows XP
Pocket Reference

David A. Karp

O'REILLY®

Beijing · Cambridge · Farnham · Köln · Paris · Sebastopol · Taipei · Tokyo

Windows XP Pocket Reference

by David A. Karp

Copyright © 2003 O'Reilly & Associates, Inc. All rights reserved.
Printed in the United States of America.

Published by O'Reilly & Associates, Inc., 1005 Gravenstein Highway North, Sebastopol, CA 95472.

O'Reilly & Associates books may be purchased for educational, business, or sales promotional use. Online editions are also available for most titles (*safari.oreilly.com*). For more information, contact our corporate/institutional sales department: (800) 998-9938 or *corporate@oreilly.com*.

Editors:	Tim O'Reilly and Nancy Kotary
Production Editor:	Linley Dolby
Cover Designer:	Ellie Volckhausen
Interior Designer:	David Futato

Printing History:

December 2002:   First Edition.

0-596-00425-7
[C]

[6/03]

Contents

Part I. Introduction

A Crash Course in the Basics of Windows XP 4
    The Desktop 4
    Point and Click 4
    Windows and Menus 6
    Files, Folders, and Disks 8
    File Types and Extensions 10

Part II. Shortcuts

Working with Files 12
    Controlling Drag-Drop 13
    Specifying the Destination 15
    Duplicating Files and Folders 16

Helpful Explorer Keystrokes 17

Keyboard Accelerators Listed by Function 19

Keyboard Accelerators Listed by Key 24

Part III. Components

Part IV. Setting Index

Alphabetical List of Windows XP Settings	92

Part V. Registry Tweaks

Registry Editor Crash Course	136
Registry Structure	137
Value Types	139
Registry Tweaks	141
Files, Folders, and File Types	141
Performance Tweaks	145
User Account and Network Settings	147
Class IDs of Interface Objects	149

Part VI. Command Prompt

Wildcards, Pipes, and Redirection	152
Command Prompt Commands	153
Windows Recovery Console	170
Recovery Console Commands	172
Lifting Recovery Console Restrictions	173

Part VII. Security Checklist

Closing Back Doors in Windows XP	176
Scan Your System for Open Ports	179
Matching a PID with a Program	179
Common TCP/IP Ports	180

PART I

Introduction

This pocket reference is intended to provide the information Windows XP users need most often in a quick and concise format. This tiny volume is small enough to fit in your pocket or laptop case, yet is packed with hundreds of tips, shortcuts, and other tidbits of information that will make Windows XP easier to use.

Enjoy quick access to keyboard and mouse shortcuts (Part II), summaries of all the programs and games included in Windows XP (Part III), and a 700-entry setting locator (Part IV). More experienced users will appreciate the most commonly used Registry tweaks (Part V), documentation on all command prompt commands (Part VI), and a security checklist (Part VII) to help protect your computer.

For less-experienced Windows XP users, a brief crash course is included at the end of this chapter. If you're a hands-on learner, you should be able to pick up any of the concepts discussed here in no time at all. Anyone wishing to learn more will benefit from the additional background and details provided by full-size books such as *Windows XP in a Nutshell*, *Windows XP Annoyances*, and *Windows Power Tools*, also available from O'Reilly.

Conventions Used in This Book

The following typographical conventions are used in this book:

Constant width

> Used to indicate anything to be typed, as well as command-line computer output, code examples, Registry keys, and keyboard accelerators (discussed below).

Constant width italic

> Used to indicate variables in examples and so-called "replaceable" text. For instance, to open a document in Notepad from the command line, you'd type notepad *filename*, where *filename* is the full path and name of the document you wish to open.

[Square brackets]

> Square brackets around an option (usually a command-line parameter) mean that the parameter is optional. Parameters and keywords not shown in square brackets are typically mandatory. If you see two or more options separated by the | character, it means that they are mutually exclusive; only one or the other can be specified, but not both.

Italic

> Used to introduce new terms and to indicate URLs, variables in text, file and folder/directory names, and UNC pathnames.

Rather than using procedural steps to tell you how to reach a given Windows XP user interface element or application, we use a shorthand path notation. For example:

> Start → Programs → Accessories → Calculator

means "Open the Start menu (on the Desktop), then choose Programs, then choose Accessories, and then click Calculator." The path is always relative to a well-known location, such as the following:

Control Panel

> Start → Control Panel (in the Windows XP–style Start Menu)
>
> Start → Settings → Control Panel (in the Classic Start Menu)

My Computer, My Network Places, Recycle Bin

> The familiar Desktop icons by these names, any of which may or may not be visible, depending on your settings

Start

> The Start button on the Taskbar

Windows Explorer/Explorer

> The two-pane folder view, commonly referred to as simply "Explorer": Start → Programs → Accessories → System Tools → Windows Explorer

xxxx menu

> Menu *xxxx* in the application currently being discussed (e.g., File, Edit)

Note that the elements of the Control Panel may or may not be divided into categories, depending on context and a setting on your computer. So, rather than a cumbersome explanation of this unfortunate design every time the Control Panel comes up, the following notation is used:

> Control Panel → [Performance and Maintenance] → Scheduled Tasks

where the category (in this case, Performance and Maintenance) is shown in square brackets, implying that you may or may not encounter this step.

TIP   There is often more than one way to reach a given application or location in the interface. You may see multiple paths to reach the same location in this book, mostly because the shortest path is not always the most convenient.

A Crash Course in the Basics of Windows XP

Windows XP, although technically an incremental upgrade to Windows 2000, has been positioned as the direct replacement to Windows Me, officially marking the end of the DOS-based Windows 9x/Me line. Windows XP is indeed the long-anticipated operating system designed to finally unify both lines of Windows, bringing the bullet-proof stability of NT to home and small business users, and the industry support of Windows 9x/Me to corporate and power users.

The following brief sections illustrate the layout of the Windows XP interface and identify the important concepts and components. Continue to Part II for tips and shortcuts for working with files, windows, and applications.

The Desktop

Like most modern operating systems that use graphical user interfaces (such as the Mac, Unix, and earlier versions of Windows), Windows XP uses the metaphor of a desktop with windows and file folders laid out on it. This desktop metaphor is provided by a program called Windows Explorer (*explorer.exe*), which runs automatically every time you start Windows. Figure 1 shows the default Windows XP Desktop.

Point and Click

Windows XP offers several settings that affect the way the interface responds to mouse clicks, all of which are documented in Part IV. The default setting (the way it works when you first install Windows XP) will also be the most familiar to most users, as it is fairly consistent with the way that most computer software works.

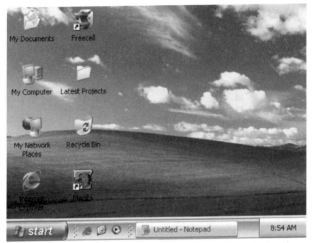

Figure 1. The layout of the Windows XP Desktop is much cleaner than previous versions

- To *click* an object, move the arrow cursor so that its pointer is over the object and press and release the left mouse button. Most buttons, menu items, checkboxes, and scrollbars are activated with single clicks.

- To *double-click* an object, click the left mouse button twice in rapid succession (not the same as clicking twice slowly). In most cases, icons require a double-click to be activated.

- *Right-click* means to click an object with the right mouse button, which typically displays the object's context menu (a list of suitable actions) rather than activating the object.

- The basic PC mouse has two buttons, but many pointing devices have more. Extra buttons can usually be configured to mimic double-clicks or even keyboard shortcuts, such as Cut, Copy, and Paste.

Windows and Menus

Any open window contains a frame with a series of standard decorations, as shown in Figure 2. To move a window from one place to another, click on the title bar and drag.

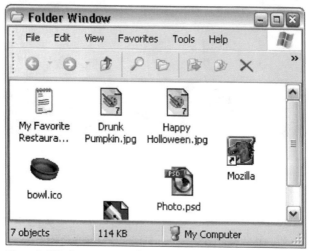

Figure 2. Windows are typically decorated with a title bar, title buttons, a menu bar, and a scrollable client area

Most types of windows are resizable, meaning that you can stretch them horizontally and vertically by grabbing an edge or a corner with the mouse. Among the buttons on most title bars are two resizing shortcuts: maximize and minimize. If you click the maximize button (the middle button in the cluster in the upper-right corner of most windows), the window will be enlarged to fill the screen, but will no longer be resizable. If you click the minimize button (the left-most button in the cluster), it will shrink out of sight and appear only as a button on the taskbar.

One or two scrollbars may appear along the bottom and far right of a window, listbox, or text input area. Scrollbars allow you to move the viewport of the window or box so that you can see all its contents. This behavior is often counterintuitive for new users because moving the scrollbar in one direction causes the window's contents to move in the opposite direction. Look at it this way: the scrollbar doesn't move the contents, it moves the *view* of the contents. Imagine a very long document with very small type. Moving the scrollbars is like moving a magnifying glass—if you move the glass down the document and look through the magnifier, it looks like the document is moving up.

If multiple windows are open, only one window has the *focus*. The window with the focus is usually the one on top of all the other windows (but not always), and is usually distinguished by a border and title that are darker in color, or otherwise distinguished from the rest. The window with the focus responds to keystrokes, although any window will respond to mouse clicks. To give a window the focus, just click on any visible portion, and it will pop to the front (be careful not to click a button or other control on the window, as the click may activate the feature in addition to bringing the window to the top of the pile). You can also click a taskbar button to activate the corresponding window (even if it's minimized), but often the most convenient method is to use the keyboard: hold the Alt key and press Tab repeatedly to cycle through open windows, and then release Alt when the desired program icon is highlighted.

Just as only one window can have the focus at any given time, only one control (text field, button, checkbox, etc.) can have the focus at any given time. Different controls show focus in different ways: pushbuttons and checkboxes have a dotted rectangle, for instance. A text field (edit box) that has the focus is not visually distinguished from the rest, but it is the only one with a blinking text cursor (insertion point). To assign the focus to a different control, just click on it, or use the Tab key (hold Shift to go backwards).

Most windows have a menu bar, commonly containing standard menu items such as File, Edit, View, and Help, as well as any application-specific menus. Click a single menu item to drop it down and then click any item in the menu as needed. Click outside of a menu or press the Esc key to get out of the menu. Figure 3 illustrates menus.

Files, Folders, and Disks

Files are the basic unit of long-term storage on a computer. Files are organized into folders (also called *directories*), which are stored on disks.

Disk names

Drives are differentiated by a single letter of the alphabet followed by a colon. "A:" and "B:" represent the first and second "floppy" (usually 3.5-inch) disk drive on the system. "C:" represents the first hard disk drive, or the first partition of the first hard disk drive. "D:" often represents a CD or DVD drive, but it (and subequent letters) can represent an additional hard disk drive or other removable drive.

Pathnames

Folders, which contain files, are stored hierarchically on a disk, folder inside folder. A path to a file begins with

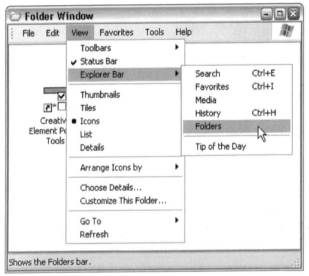

Figure 3. Menus are easy to use, but nested menus can be cumbersome

the root (top-level) directory, represented as the drive letter followed by a sole backslash (e.g., *C:*). Additional nested folders are simply listed after their "parents," with backslashes used to separate each folder; for example, *C:\ Windows\System32* represents the *System32* folder, located in the *Windows* folder, located in the root of drive *C:*. The heirarchy of all the folders on your hard disk is visually represented by the tree in the left pane of Windows Explorer, discussed in Part III.

Network paths

Files and folders accessed remotely over a network are referred to via a UNC (Universal Naming Convention) pathname, similar to the standard path notation discussed previously. For example, the UNC path *\\shoebox\ o\hemp\adriana.txt* refers to a file named *adrianna.txt*, located in the *hemp* folder, located on drive *o:*, located on a computer named "shoebox."

Long filenames

DOS and Windows 3.1, the Microsoft operating systems that preceded Windows 95 and Windows NT/XP, only supported filenames with a maximum of eight characters, plus a three-character file type extension (e.g., *myfile.txt*). Filenames could further only be composed of letters, numbers, and these basic symbols: $ % ^ ' ` - _ @ ~ ! ( ) # &. Spaces were not allowed.

Windows XP supports long filenames (up to 260 characters), which can include spaces, as well as the additional punctuation characters: $ % ^ ' ` - _ @ ~ ! ( ) # & + , ; = [ ], and extensions are no longer limited to three characters; for example, *.html* is perfectly valid (and distinctly different from *.htm*).

NOTE

Windows XP's filesystem is case-preserving, but also case-insensitive. For example, the case of a file named *FooBar.txt* will be preserved with the capital F and B, but if you were to type FOObar in a File → Open dialog box, Windows would recognize it as the same file.

File Types and Extensions

Most files have a filename extension, the (usually three) letters that appear after the last dot in any file's name. Common file extensions include *.xls* (for Excel spreadsheets), *.txt* (for plain text files), *.html* (for hypertext markup language files, commonly known as web pages), and *.jpg* (for JPEG image files). Although all these files hold very different types of data, the only way Windows differentiates them is by their filename extensions.

By default, file extensions are hidden, but it's best to have them displayed. Go to Control Panel → Folder Options → View tab, and clear the checkbox next to the "Hide extensions for known file types" option. This way, you can see what type a given file is, and even change its extension to expose new functionality.

WARNING

Renaming a file's extension will not alter the file's internal structure or formatting; you'll need an application that understands the file's format to convert it to a different type. However, changing the extension will likely change the application with which the file is associated.

Windows uses a file's extension to determine what to do when the file is double-clicked and right-clicked; this system is known as file types or file associations. To see all the configured file extensions on your system, go to Control Panel → Folder Options → File Types tab. Here, you can change the applications that are associated with certain documents, and even add new associations and functionality.

TIP   Although only the *default* application for a file type will be used when a file is double-clicked, additional programs can be linked up with a file type so that they appear when a file is right-clicked. For example, you can set it up so that right-clicking a *jpg* image file allows you to quickly view, edit, print, or email the image by simply selecting the appropriate action.

PART II

Shortcuts

There are a bunch of ways to improve your experience with
Windows XP. Some solutions involve making modifications
and additions to the operating system, while others describe
how to work with the tools that come out of the box. The
tips in this chapter illustrate the various keyboard and mouse
shortcuts available in Windows XP.

Working with Files

The tips that follow show you how to predict—and even
change—how Explorer responds to the dragging and dropping of files. Here's an overview of how drag-drop works in
Windows Explorer:

- If you drag an object from one place to another on the
  same physical drive (*c:\docs* to *c:\files*), the object is moved.

- If you drag an object from one physical drive to another
  physical drive (*c:\docs* to *d:\files*), the object is copied,
  resulting in two identical files on your system. This means
  that if you drag an object from one physical drive to
  another physical drive and then back to the first physical
  drive, but in a different folder (*c:\docs* to *d:\files* to *c:\stuff*),
  you'll end up with three copies of the object.

- If you drag *any* file named *setup.exe* or *install.exe* from
  one place to another, Windows will create a shortcut to
  the file, regardless of the source or destination folder. The
  exception is if you drag a file named *setup.exe* into a

recordable CD drive, it will be copied. And if you drag a bunch of files of different types (including, say, *setup.exe*), the create-a-shortcut rules will be ignored, and they'll just be copied or moved as appropriate.

- If you drag any file with the *.exe* filename extension into any portion of your Start Menu or into any subfolder of your *Start Menu* folder, Windows will create a shortcut to the file. Dragging other file types (documents, script files, other shortcuts) to the Start Menu will simply move or copy them there, according to the aforementioned rules.

- If you drag a system object (such as a Control Panel icon), a warning is displayed, and a shortcut to the item is created. These objects aren't actually files and can't be duplicated or removed from their original locations.

TIP   To aid in learning the keystrokes, notice that the mouse cursor changes depending on the action taken. A small plus sign [+] appears when copying, and a curved arrow appears when creating a shortcut. If you see no symbol, the object will be moved. This visual feedback is very important; it can prevent mistakes if you pay attention to it.

Controlling Drag-Drop

The best way to control drag-drop is to use a combination of certain keystrokes and the correct mouse button to ensure the desired results every time you drag an object. That way, you don't have to try to predict what will happen based on some rules you won't likely remember.

Copy

To copy an object in any situation, hold the Ctrl key while dragging. If you press Ctrl *before* you click, Windows assumes you're still selecting files (as Ctrl is also used to select multiple files, as described later in this chapter), so make sure to press it only *after* you've started dragging but before you let go of that mouse button. Of course, this won't work for system objects such as Control Panel items—a shortcut will be created regardless. Using the Ctrl key in this way also works when dragging a file from one part of a folder to another part of the same folder.

Move

To *move* an object in any situation, hold the Shift key while dragging. Likewise, if you press Shift before you click, Windows assumes you're still selecting files, so make sure you press it after you've started dragging but before you let go of that mouse button. Like above, this doesn't apply to system objects like Control Panel icons.

Create a shortcut

To create a shortcut to an object under any situation, hold the Alt key while dragging. Note that this is different than in previous versions of Windows.

Choose what happens each time

To choose what happens to dragged files each time *without* having to press any keys, drag your files with the *right mouse button*, and a special menu will appear when the files are dropped. This context menu is especially helpful, because it displays only options appropriate to the type of object you're dragging and the place where you've dropped it.

Undo

Explorer's Undo command (in the Edit menu, as well as available by right-clicking in an empty area of Explorer or the Desktop, or by pressing Ctrl-Z) allows you to undo the last few file operations. If you've copied, moved, or renamed one or more objects, the command will read Undo Copy, Undo Move, or Undo Rename, respectively. Additionally, if your Recycle Bin is configured to store files, Undo Delete may appear.

| TIP | If you're doing a lot of copying, moving, and delet-
ing of files, it's hard to know exactly what you're
undoing when you use Undo. The easiest way to tell
is to click and hold the mouse button over the Undo
menu item in Explorer or a single-folder window
and look in the status bar (use View → Status Bar if
it's not visible). This is not available on the Desktop, but luckily, Undo works the same regardless of
the folder from which you use it. |
| --- | --- |

Specifying the Destination

Typically, you must have both the source folder and the destination folder open and visible to copy or move an object.
Here are some ways to overcome this limitation:

- Open Explorer (launch *Explorer.exe*) or a single folder
  window (by double-clicking a folder icon) and make sure
  the folder tree is visible (View → Explorer Bar → Folders). Or, right-click any folder icon and select Explore.
  Then, drag one or more items over the tree pane on the
  left and hold the mouse cursor over the visible branch of
  the destination folder. After two or three seconds,
  Explorer automatically expands the branch and makes
  the subfolders visible. Figure 4 illustrates this.

- You can also use cut-and-paste (or copy-and-paste) to
  move or copy files, respectively. Select the file(s) you
  want to copy, right-click, and select Copy to copy the
  file(s) or Cut to move the file(s). The keyboard shortcuts
  for the cut, copy, and paste operations are Ctrl-X, Ctrl-C,
  and Ctrl-V, respectively. Then, open the destination
  folder (or click on the Desktop), right-click on an empty
  area (or open the Edit menu), and select Paste. Whether
  the file is copied or moved—or a shortcut is made—
  depends on the same criteria as if you had dragged and
  dropped the item.

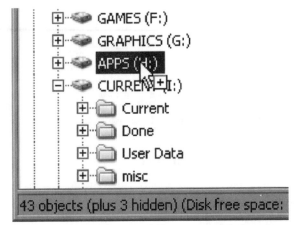

Figure 4. Hold dragged files over folders to expand the branches

- The standard Windows Explorer toolbar has two buttons, Move To and Copy To, that allow you to point to a location when moving and copying, respectively. Select the file(s) you want to move or copy, click Move To or Copy To, and then specify the destination folder in the dialog that appears.

  Unfortunately, these functions can't be found in Explorer's menus or in the context menus of any files or folders; they're only available on the toolbar. If Explorer's toolbar isn't currently visible, go to View → Toolbars → Standard Buttons to turn it on. By default, the Move To and Copy To buttons are in the sixth and seventh positions on the toolbar, respectively. If they're not, right-click on the toolbar and select Customize. An alternative tool with more options is available as part of Creative Element Power Tools (*http://www.creativelement.com/powertools/*).

Duplicating Files and Folders

Windows lets you copy and move files from one folder to another by dragging them with different combinations of keystrokes, as described earlier in this chapter. You can also rename a file by clicking on its name or highlighting it and pressing the F2 key. However, if you want to make a duplicate of a file in the s*ame* directory and assign it a different name, the process might not be as obvious. There are several ways to do it:

- Hold the Ctrl key while dragging a file from one part of the window to another part of the *same* window. This works in single-folder windows, on the Desktop, and in Explorer.

- Use the right mouse button to drag the file from one part of the window to another part of the same window, and then select Copy Here.

- For keyboard enthusiasts: press Ctrl-C and then Ctrl-V to create a duplicate of a file using the clipboard.

Regardless of which solution you use, duplicates are always assigned new names to avoid conflicts.

If you need a bunch of duplicates of a file or folder, start by duplicating it once. Then, select both the original and the copy, and duplicate them both. Then, select the resulting four objects and duplicate them to make eight.

Helpful Explorer Keystrokes

Certain keyboard shortcuts can be real time savers in Explorer, especially when used in conjunction with the mouse. The following tips assume you're using standard double-clicking, the default in Windows XP. If you've chosen to have icons respond to a single click (by going to Control Panel → Folder Options → General tab), just replace "double-click" here with "single-click."

- Hold the Alt key while double-clicking on a file or folder to view the Properties sheet for that object.

Although this is often quicker than right-clicking and selecting Properties, the right-click menu—also known as the context menu—has a bunch of other options, most of which are not accessible with keystrokes. For more information on context menus and file types, see the discussion of Explorer in Part III.

- Hold the Shift key while double-clicking a folder icon to open an Explorer window at that location (as opposed to a single-folder window). Be careful when using this, because Shift is also used to select multiple files. The best way is to select the file first.

- Press Backspace in an open folder window or in Explorer to go to the parent folder.

- Hold Alt while pressing the left arrow (cursor) key to navigate to the previously viewed folder. Note that this is not necessarily the parent folder, but rather the last folder in Explorer's history. Once you've returned to a previously viewed folder, you can also hold Alt while pressing the right arrow key to move in the opposite direction (i.e., forward). Explorer's toolbar also has Back and Next buttons by default, which work just like their counterparts in Internet Explorer.

- With the focus on Explorer's folder tree, use the left and right arrow keys to collapse and expand folders, respectively. Press the asterisk (*) key to expand all the subfolders of the currently selected branch.

- Hold the Shift key while clicking on the close button [X] to close all open folder windows in the chain that was used to get to that folder. (This, of course, makes sense only in the single-folder view and with the Open each folder in its own window option turned on.)

- Select one icon, then hold the Shift key while clicking on another icon in the same folder to select it and all the items in between.

- Hold the Ctrl key to select or deselect multiple files or folders, one by one. Note that you can't select more than one folder in the folder tree pane of Explorer, but you can in the right pane.

You can also use Ctrl key to modify your selection. For example, if you've used the Shift key or a rubber band to select the several files in a folder, you can hold Ctrl while clicking or dragging a second rubber band to invert selections (highlighting additional files or deselecting already-highlighed files) *without* losing your original selection.

- Press Ctrl-A to quickly select all the contents of a folder: both files and folders.
- In Explorer or any single-folder window (even in the folder tree pane), press a letter key to quickly jump to the first file or folder starting with that letter. Continue typing to jump further. For example, pressing the T key in your *Windows* folder will jump to the *Tasks* subfolder. Press T again to jump to the next object that starts with T. Or, press T and then quickly press A to skip all the Ts and jump to *taskman.exe*. If there's enough of a delay between the T and the A keys, Explorer will forget about the T and you'll jump to the first entry that starts with A.

Keyboard Accelerators Listed by Function

The following keys operate in most contexts—i.e., on the Desktop, in Explorer, and within most applications and dialogs.

Action	Key(s)
AutoPlay, disable temporarily	Shift (while inserting CD)
Checkbox, toggle on or off	Spacebar
Clipboard, copy	Ctrl-C
Clipboard, copy current window as a bitmap	Alt-PrintScreen
Clipboard, copy entire screen as a bitmap	PrintScreen
Clipboard, cut	Ctrl-X
Clipboard, paste	Ctrl-V
Close current document	Ctrl-F4
Close current window	Alt-F4
Close dialog box, message window, or menu	Esc
Command button, click	Spacebar
Context menu, open	Shift-F10, or context menu key on some keyboards
Controls, cycle focus on a dialog box	Tab (hold Shift to go in reverse)
Copy selected item or selected text to the clipboard	Ctrl-C
Cut selected item or selected text to the clipboard	Ctrl-X
Date and Time Properties, open	⊞-B, Spacebar
Delete a file without putting it in the Recycle Bin	Shift-Del or Shift-drag item to Recycle Bin
Delete selected item	Del
Desktop, activate	Ctrl-Esc (or ⊞), then Esc, Tab, Tab, Tab
Desktop, activate by minimizing all windows	⊞-D, or click empty portion of Taskbar and press Alt-M
Dialog box, cycle through controls	Tab (hold Shift to go in reverse)
Dialog box, cycle through tabs	Ctrl-Tab (hold Shift to go in reverse)
Dialog box, click OK	Enter (or Return)
Dialog box, click Cancel	Esc
Document, close	Ctrl-F4

Action	Key(s)
Document, move to the beginning	Ctrl-Home
Document, move to the end	Ctrl-End
Document, switch between	Ctrl-F6 or Ctrl-Tab
Drop-down listbox, open	Down Arrow or F4
Exit an application	Alt-F4
Exit Windows	Ctrl-Esc, then Alt-F4
File, delete without moving to Recycle Bin	Shift-Del
File, search	⊞-F (or F3 or Ctrl-F in Windows Explorer or on the Desktop)
Find a computer on your network	Ctrl-⊞-F
Find Files or Folders	⊞-F (or F3 or Ctrl-F in Windows Explorer or on the Desktop)
Focus, move between controls on a dialog box	Tab (hold Shift to go in reverse)
Folder, close current and all parents (Windows Explorer in single-folder view only)	Shift-click Close button
Folder, expand and collapse folders in tree	Right and left arrows
Folder, open in two-pane Explorer view	Shift–double-click
Folder, search	⊞-F (or F3 or Ctrl-F in Windows Explorer or on the Desktop)
Help (in most applications)	F1
Help and Support Services, open	⊞-F1
Icon, Activate selected	Enter (or Return)
Icon, view Properties of selected	Alt-Enter (or Alt-Return)
Listbox, drop-down	Down Arrow or F4
Listbox, select multiple items	Ctrl-click
Listbox, select or deselected items	Ctrl-Spacebar
Lock computer	⊞-L (or press Ctrl-Alt-Del and then Spacebar)
Menu, activate selected item	Enter (or Return)

Action	Key(s)
Menu, activate specific item with letter *x* underlined	Alt-*x* if menu doesn't have focus, *x* by itself if menu has focus
Menu, basic navigation	Arrow keys
Menu, close	Esc
Menu, move focus to	F10 or Alt (by itself)
Menu, open context menu	Shift-F10, or context menu key on some keyboards
Minimize all windows and move focus to Desktop	⊞-D, or click empty portion of Taskbar and press Alt-M
Minimize current window	⊞-M (hold Shift to undo)
Panes, move focus between	F6
Parent folder, move to (in Windows Explorer)	Backspace
Paste the contents of the clipboard	Ctrl-V
Properties, display for an icon	Alt–double-click, or select and then press Alt-Enter
Refresh (in Windows Explorer, on the Desktop, and some other applications)	F5
Rename selected icon or file in Windows Explorer or on the Desktop	F2
Run (same as Start → Run)	⊞-R
Screenshot, copy current window as a bitmap to the clipboard	Alt-PrintScreen
Screenshot, copy entire screen as a bitmap to the clipboard	PrintScreen
Scroll down one screen	Page Down
Scroll up one screen	Page Up
Scroll without moving selection	Ctrl-arrow key
Search for a computer on your network	Ctrl-⊞-F
Search for Files or Folders	⊞-F
Search for Files or Folders (in Windows Explorer or on the Desktop only)	F3 or Ctrl-F
Select all	Ctrl-A

Action	Key(s)
Shortcut, create	Alt-drag file
Start Menu, open	⊞ or Ctrl-Esc
Switch to next application	Alt-Tab or Ctrl-Esc (hold Shift to go in reverse)
Switch to next document window	Ctrl-F6 or Ctrl-Tab (hold Shift to go in reverse)
System menu, show for current document	Alt-hyphen
System menu, show for current window	Alt-Spacebar
System Properties, open	⊞-Pause/Break
Tabs, switch between tabs	Ctrl-Tab (hold Shift to go in reverse)
Task Manager, open	Shift-Ctrl-Esc (or press Ctrl-Alt-Del and click Task Manager)
Taskbar and Start Menu Properties, open	Ctrl-Esc, then Alt-Enter
Taskbar buttons, cycle through	⊞-Tab
Undo	Ctrl-Z
Window, activate next	Alt-Tab (hold Shift to go in reverse)
Window, close	Alt-F4
Window, drop to bottom of pile	Alt-Esc
Window, minimize	⊞-M (hold Shift to undo)
Window, minimize all	⊞-D (hold Shift to undo)
Window, switch to	Alt-Tab (hold Shift to go in reverse)
Windows Explorer, open	⊞-E
Windows Explorer, switch between panes	F6

Note also that there are essentially limitless combinations of
keystrokes that can be used to activate any particular feature
in a given application, all of which can be formed by combining the various keystrokes listed here, especially when using
Alt-*x*, where *x* is the underlined character in a menu or dialog
box. For example, you can press Alt-F to open an application's File menu, then press P to Print, then press Enter to
begin printing. Or, press Ctrl-Esc to open the Start Menu, Alt-

Enter to open Taskbar and Start Menu Properties, Ctrl-Tab to open the Taskbar tab (if necessary), and Alt-L to lock (or unlock) the Taskbar.

Keyboard Accelerators Listed by Key

The following keystrokes work in Windows Explorer and most of the components that come with Windows XP. However, some applications (including Microsoft applications) don't always follow the rules.

Key	Action
F1	Start Help (supported in most applications)
F2	Rename selected icon or file in Windows Explorer or on the Desktop
F3	Open a Search window (in Windows Explorer or on the Desktop only)
F4	Open a drop-down list (supported in many dialog boxes)—for example, press F4 in a File Open dialog to drop down the Look In list
F5	Refresh the view in Windows Explorer, on the Desktop, in the Registry Editor, and in some other applications
F6	Move focus between panes in Windows Explorer
F10	Send focus to the current application's menu
Arrow keys	Basic navigation: move through menus, reposition the text cursor (insertion point), change the file selection, and so on
Backspace	Move up one level in folder hierarchy (Windows Explorer only)
Delete	Delete selected item(s) or selected text
Down Arrow	Open a drop-down listbox
End	Go to end of line when editing text, or end of file list
Enter	Activate highlighted choice in menu or dialog box, or insert a carriage return when editing text
Esc	Close dialog box, message window, or menu without activating any choice (usually the same as clicking Cancel)
Home	Go to beginning of line (when editing text), or beginning of file list
Page Down	Scroll down one screen

Key	Action
Page Up	Scroll up one screen
PrintScreen	Copy entire screen as a bitmap to the clipboard
Spacebar	Toggle a checkbox that is selected in a dialog box, activate the command button with the focus, or toggle the selection of files when selecting multiple files with Ctrl
Tab	Move focus to next control in a dialog box or window (hold Shift to go backwards)
Alt (by itself)	Send focus to the menu (same as F10)
Alt-*x*	Activate menu or dialog control, where letter *x* is underlined
Alt–double-click (on icon)	Display Properties sheet
Alt-Enter	Display Properties sheet for selected icon in Windows Explorer or on the Desktop; also switches command prompt between windowed and full screen display
Alt-Esc	Drop active window to bottom of pile, which, in effect, activates next open window
Alt-F4	Close current window; if Taskbar or Desktop has the focus, exit Windows
Alt-hyphen	Open the current document's system menu in an MDI (multiple document interface) application
Alt-numbers	When used with the numbers on the numeric keypad only, inserts special characters corresponding to their ASCII codes into many applications; for example, type Alt-0169 for the copyright symbol (see "Character Map" in Part III)
Alt-PrintScreen	Copy active window as a bitmap to the clipboard
Alt-Shift-Tab	Same as Alt-Tab, but in the opposite direction
Alt-Spacebar	Open the current window's system menu
Alt-Tab, Tab	Switch to the next running application—hold Shift while pressing Tab to cycle through running applications
Alt-M	When the Taskbar has the focus, minimize all windows and move focus to the Desktop
Alt-S	When the Taskbar has the focus, open the Start Menu
Ctrl-A	Select all; in Windows Explorer, selects all files in the current folder; in word processors, selects all text in the current document

Key	Action
Ctrl-Alt-*x*	User-defined accelerator for a shortcut, where *x* is any key (discussed at the beginning of this chapter)
Ctrl-Alt-Del	Show the logon dialog when no user is currently logged on; otherwise, switch to the Windows Security dialog, which provides access to Task Manager and Shut Down, as well as allows you to change your password or lock the computer; use Ctrl-Alt-Del to access Task Manager when Explorer crashes or your computer becomes unresponsive
Ctrl-arrow key	Scroll without moving selection
Ctrl-click	Used to select multiple, noncontiguous items in a list or in Windows Explorer
Ctrl-drag	Copy a file (discussed earlier in this chapter)
Ctrl-End	Move to the end of a document (in many applications)
Ctrl-Esc	Open the Start Menu; press Esc and then Tab to then move focus to the Taskbar, or Tab again to move focus to the Desktop
Ctrl-F4	Close a document window in an MDI application
Ctrl-F6	Switch between multiple documents in an MDI (multiple document interface) application; similar to Ctrl-Tab; hold Shift to go in reverse
Ctrl-Home	Move to the beginning of a document (in many applications)
Ctrl-Spacebar	Select or deselect multiple, non-contiguous items in a listbox or in Windows Explorer
Ctrl-Tab	Switch between tabs in a tabbed dialog, or between multiple documents in an MDI application (similar to Ctrl-F6, except that Ctrl-Tab doesn't work in most word processors); hold Shift to go in reverse
Ctrl-C	Copy the selected item or selected text to the clipboard (also interrupts some command-prompt applications)
Ctrl-F	Open a Search window (in Windows Explorer or on the Desktop only)
Ctrl-V	Paste the contents of the clipboard
Ctrl-X	Cut the selected item or selected text to the clipboard
Ctrl-Z	Undo; for example, erases text just entered and repeats the last file operation in Windows Explorer
Shift	While inserting a CD, hold to disable AutoPlay.
Shift-arrow keys	Select text or select multiple items in a listbox or in Windows Explorer

Key	Action
Shift-click	Select all items between currently selected item and item on which you're clicking; also works when selecting text
Shift-click Close button	Close current folder and all parent folders (Windows Explorer in single-folder view only)
Shift-Alt-Tab	Same as Alt-Tab, but in reverse
Shift-Ctrl-Tab	Same as Ctrl-Tab, but in reverse
Shift-Ctrl-Esc	Open Task Manager (see Part III)
Shift-Del	Delete a file without putting it in the Recycle Bin
Shift-double-click	Open folder in two-pane Explorer view
Shift-Tab	Same as Tab, but in reverse
⊞	Open the Start Menu
⊞-F1	Start Help and Support Services
⊞-Tab	Cycle through taskbar buttons without activating the applications (Alt-Tab is more convenient, though)
⊞-Pause/Break	Display System Properties dialog
⊞-B, Spacebar	Open Date and Time Properties (see Part III)
⊞-D	Minimize all windows and move focus to Desktop (buggy on some systems; if your Desktop turns gray, use the Task Manager to close *Explorer.exe*)
Shift-⊞-D	Undo minimize all
⊞-E	Start Windows Explorer
⊞-F	Search for Files or Folders
Ctrl-⊞-F	Search for a computer on your network
⊞-L	Lock computer, requiring password to regain access (you can also lock your computer by pressing Ctrl-Alt-Del and clicking Lock Computer)
⊞-M	Minimize current window
Shift-⊞-M	Undo minimize current window
⊞-R	Display Run dialog (same as Start → Run)
⊞-U	Open the Utility Manager (see Part III)

Key	Action
Left/Right arrow	Move cursor back/forward one character
Ctrl-Left/Right arrow	Move cursor back/forward one word
Home/End	Move cursor to beginning/end of line
Up/Down arrow	Scroll up (and back) through list of stored commands (called the command buffer or history). Each press of the Up key recalls the previous command and displays it on the command line
Page Up/Down	Recall oldest/most recent command in buffer
Insert	Toggle insert/overtype mode (block cursor implies overtype mode)
Esc	Erase current line
F1	Repeat text typed in previous line, one character at a time
F2-*key*	Repeat text typed in previous line, up to first character matching *key*
F3	Repeat text typed in previous line
F4-*key*	Delete characters from present character position up to (but not including) *key* (does not work reliably in Windows XP)
F5	Change the template for F1, F2, and F3 (described above) so that earlier commands are used as the template; press F5 repeatedly to cycle through the entire command buffer
F6	Place an end-of-file character (^Z) at current position of command line
F7	Show all entries in command buffer (history)
Alt-F7	Clear all entries in command buffer (history)
chars-F8	Entering one or more characters *chars* followed by F8 will display the most recent entry in the command buffer beginning with *chars*. Pressing F8 again will display the next most recent matching command, and so on. If no characters are specified, F8 simply cycles through existing commands in buffer.
F9-*command#*	Display designated command on command line; use F7 to obtain numbers
Ctrl-C	Interrupt the output of most command prompt applications

PART III

Components

This chapter provides an alphabetical reference to all the useful components that make up Windows XP: an encyclopedia, if you will, of everything you can do with Windows out of the box. Some of the more prominent applications and utilities that come with Windows XP are available through shortcuts on the Start Menu, but many useful tools aren't as conspicuous, available only to those who know where to look.

In Windows, there is usually more than one way to accomplish any task. So, each entry in this chapter starts with the formal name of the component as it appears on screen and the executable filename, which can be typed in the address bar, the command prompt, or in Start → Run. Then, its location in the interface (if applicable) is shown with standard path notation, followed by a description, tips, command-line options, or other applicable helpful information.

Accessibility Options   \windows\system\access.cpl
Control Panel → [Accessibility Options] → Accessibility Options

This dialog provides options for the accessibility tools in Windows XP, such as StickyKeys, FilterKeys, ToggleKeys, MouseKeys, SoundSentry, and other settings designed to make a computer easier to use for those with poor eyesight, hearing, or some other physical challenge.

Accessibility Wizard   *\windows\system32\accwiz.exe*

Start → All Programs → Accessories → Accessibility → Accessibility Wizard

The Accessibility Wizard is an alternate interface to the settings
provided in the Accessibility Options dialog, in that it will walk
you through the available options one by one, lending assistance
where you may not otherwise know which options you need.

Activate Windows   *\windows\system32\oobe\msoobe.exe*

Start → Settings → Activate Windows

Microsoft's copy-protection scheme works as follows: Windows
combines the 25-character CD Key you typed during the installation of Windows XP installation, along with an 8-digit hardware
ID (based on values taken from your display adapter, SCSI
adapter, IDE adapter, network adapter, memory amount,
processor, hard drive, and CD/DVD drive), and then transmits
this information to Microsoft. In return, a 42-digit Confirmation
ID is returned and used to activate your copy of Windows XP.

Active Connections Utility   *\windows\system32\netstat.exe*

This tool displays protocol statistics and current TCP/IP network
connections. See "Scan your System for Open Ports" in Part VII
for an example. Type netstat by itself to list the active incoming
and outgoing network connections, or use these options:

```
netstat [-a] [-e] [-nc] [-o] [-p proto] [-r] [-s]
[interval]
```

Option	Description
-a	Display all connections and open ports.
-e	Display Ethernet statistics; can be combined with -s.
-n	Display addresses and ports in numerical format (e.g. 192.168.0.1:88).
-o	Display the process that owns each listed connection.
-p proto	Show the connections corresponding the protocol; proto can be IP, IPv6, ICMP, ICMPv6, TCP, TCPv6, UDP, or UDPv6.

Option	Description
-r	Display the routing table.
-s	Display statistics for each protocol. By default, statistics are shown for all protocols, but this can be filtered with the -p option.
interval	Repeatedly run netstat, pausing *interval* seconds between each display. Press Ctrl-C to stop the display at any time. If omitted, netstat will display the current statistics once and then quit.

Add Hardware Wizard

\windows\system\hdwwiz.cpl

Control Panel → Add Hardware

When you turn on your computer, Windows automatically scans for any newly added plug-and-play devices and installs drivers for any it finds. If you're trying to install a device that isn't detected automatically, you'll need to run the Add Hardware Wizard.

Add or Remove Programs

\windows\system32\appwiz.cpl

Control Panel → Add or Remove Programs

This dialog allows you to uninstall applications and add or remove Windows XP components. Click Change or Remove Programs to view a list of all your installed applications, and optionally uninstall or modify any item in the list. Click Add New Programs to launch the file, *setup.exe*, in your floppy drive or CD drive. Or, choose Add/Remove Windows Components to add or remove any of the optional programs that come with Windows XP.

Address Book

\program files\outlook express\wab.exe

Start → All Programs → Accessories → Address Book
Start → Search → For People
Outlook Express → Tools menu → Address Book

The Address Book is a database containing names, addresses, and other contact information, used by Outlook Express and a handful of other applications. The main window in the Address Book is set up somewhat like Explorer, with a hierarchical view of folders in the left pane, and a list of addresses contained in the currently selected folder in the right pane. To add a new entry to your Address Book, select New Contact from the File menu, or right-click an empty area of the right pane, and select New, and then New Contact.

At

"At" is the command-line interface to the Scheduled Tasks feature, discussed later in this chapter, and is used to schedule commands and programs to run on a computer at a specified time and date. The syntax is as follows:

```
at [\\computer] time [/interactive] [/every:date]
    [/next:date] "command"
at [\\computer] [id] [/delete] [/yes]
```

Option	Description
\\computer	Specify the name of a remote computer on the network to add the new task to that computer's scheduled tasks list.
time	The time of day to run the task, specified in 24-hour (military) time.
/interactive	If you omit the /interactive option, the task will be run invisibly in the background. Use caution when starting background processes, however, as you won't be able to interact with them at all, other than closing them with Task Manager.
/every:date /next:date	By default, At creates one-time tasks, executed only on the date in which they were created. To specify the day or range of days, use the /every or /next options.
/delete	Use /delete to remove one or all tasks originally created with At. Specify the aforementioned task ID to end that task, or omit the ID to delete all tasks.
/yes	Include /yes to bypass the prompt that appears when you attempt to delete all tasks.

Examples

Run Disk Defragmenter at 11:15 P.M. every Thursday:

```
at 23:15 /every:thursday dfrg.msc
```

Run Disk Defragmenter at 11:15 A.M. on the 21st day of every month:

```
at 11:15 /every:21 dfrg.msc
```

Run Solitaire at 3:45 in the afternoon, Tuesdays and Thursdays:

```
at 15:45 /interactive /every:tuesday,thursday sol
```

Run chkdsk at 6:33 P.M. next Saturday only:

```
at 18:33 /next:saturday chkdsk
```

Attrib
\windows\system32\attrib.exe

Attrib allows you to change the file and folder attributes from the command line, settings otherwise only available in a file's or folder's Properties window. The attributes can be thought of as switches, independently turned on or off for any file or group of files. Attrib is used as follows:

```
attrib [+r|-r] [+a|-a] [+s|-s] [+h|-h] [filename]
```

Option	Description
r	(read-only) Turn on the read-only attribute of a file or folder to protect it from accidental deletion or modification.
a	(archive) The archive attribute has no effect on how a file is used, but is automatically turned on when a file is modified or created.
s	(system) Files with the system attribute are typically used to to boot the computer.
h	(hidden) To hide any file or folder from plain view in Explorer or on the Desktop, turn on its hidden attribute.

For example, to hide a file, type attrib +h *filename*. To turn off the hidden attribute and simultaneously turn on the archive attribute, type attrib -h +a *filename*.

Backup
\windows\system32\ntbackup.exe

Start → All Programs → Accessories → System Tools → Backup

Backup copies files from your hard drive to a tape drive, second hard drive, or other removable storage device for the purpose of safeguarding or archiving your data. Microsoft Backup works by creating a backup set, or a collection of selected files to be backed up to a removable storage device. This backup set, along with all the selected options available in Backup are known collectively as a backup "job." To begin creating a backup job, choose the Backup tab, and use the familiar Explorer-like two-pane view to navigate through your folders. Click on the checkbox next to any object to select it for backup, and then click Start Backup when you're done.

> **TIP** In Windows XP Professional, Backup is installed through Add or Remove Programs. In Windows XP Home, you'll need to open the *\valueadd\msft\ ntbackup* folder on your Windows CD and double-click the *Ntbackup.msi* file to install the software.

Boot Configuration Manager   *\windows\system32\bootcfg.exe*

The Windows XP Boot Manager is responsible for supporting multiple operating systems on the same system. The Boot Configuration Manager, included only with Windows XP Professional, is used to configure and view entries in the Boot Manager configuration file (*boot.ini*). The syntax is as follows:

```
bootcfg /command [parameters]
```

Among the commands available to the Boot Configuration Manager, the more interesting are the /copy, /delete, and /query commands, used to add, remove, and view the entries in *boot.ini*, respectively. The /query command is the default; if you simply type bootcfg with no parameter, it's the same as typing bootcfg /query. Type bootcfg /? to see a list of all commands.

Calculator   *\windows\system32\calc.exe*

Start → All Programs → Accessories → Calculator

Data can be entered by clicking the buttons or by pressing keys on the keyboard. All keys have keyboard equivalents; those key mappings that are not quite obvious (such as log) are documented in Table 1. Note that many of the functions are available only in Scientific mode (Table 2).

Table 1. Calculations and keyboard equivalents

Calc button	Keyboard key	Action
C	Esc	Clear all calculations
CE	Del	Clear last entry
Back	Backspace	Clear last digit
MR	Ctrl-R	Display the number stored in memory
MS	Ctrl-M	Store the current value in memory
M+	Ctrl-P	Add the current value to the number stored in memory
MC	Ctrl-L	Clear the Memory
+/-	F9	Change the sign (negative)

Table 2. Scientific calculation buttons and keyboard equivalents

Calc button	Keyboard key	Action
Inv	i	Sets the inverse function for sin, cos, tan, PI, x^y, x^2, x^3, Ln, log, sum, and s.
Hyp	h	Sets the hyperbolic function for sin, cos, and tan.
F-E	v	Turns scientific notation on and off. Can only be used with decimal numbers. Numbers larger than 10^{15} are always displayed with exponents.
( )	( )	Starts and ends a new level of parentheses. The maximum number of nested parentheses is 25. The current number of levels appears in the box above the) button.
dms	m	if the displayed number is in degrees, convert to degree-minute-second format. Use Inv + dms to reverse the operation.
Exp	x	The next digit(s) entered constitute the exponent. The exponent cannot be larger than 289. Decimal only.
Ln	n	Natural (base e) logarithm. Inv + Ln calculates e raised to the nth power, where n is the current number.
sin	s	Sine of the displayed number. Inv + sin gives arc sine. Hyp + sin gives hyperbolic sine. Inv + Hyp + sin gives arc hyperbolic sine.
x^y	y	x to the yth power. Inv + x^y calculates the yth root of x.
Log	l	The common (base 10) logarithm. Inv + log yields 10 to the xth power, where x is the displayed number.

Table 2. Scientific calculation buttons and keyboard equivalents

Calc button	Keyboard key	Action
Cos	o	Cosine of the displayed number. Inv + cosin gives arc cosine. Hyp + cosin gives hyperbolic cosine. Inv + Hyp + cosin gives arc hyperbolic cosine.
x^3	#	Cubes the displayed number. Inv + x^3 gives the cube root.
n!	!	Factorial of the displayed number.
tan	t	Tangent of the displayed number. Inv + tan gives arc tan. Hyp + tan gives hyperbolic tan. Inv + Hyp + tan gives arc hyperbolic tan.
x^2	@	Squares the displayed number. Inv + x^2 gives the square root.
l/x	r	Reciprocal of displayed number.
Pi	p	The value of *pi* (3.1415...). Inv + Pi gives 2 × pi.

Character Map   \windows\system32\charmap.exe

Start → All Programs → Accessories → System Tools → Character Map

Character Map displays a visual map of all the characters in any font, making it easy to access symbols not otherwise accessible with the keyboard. Any characters can then be copied and pasted into other documents.

Chkdsk   \windows\system32\chkdsk.exe

Chkdsk scans the disk surface, checks the integrity of files and folders, and looks for lost clusters (among other things), correcting any problems that are found, and sometimes even freeing disk space consumed by unusable fragments of data. To use chkdsk effectively, include the following optional parameters:

    chkdsk [drive[filename]] [/f] [/r] [/x] [/i] [/c] [/v]

Option	Description
/f	Fix any errors found. If /f is omitted, errors are merely reported, and no changes to the disk are made.
/r	Locates bad sectors and recovers readable information.

Option	Description
/x	Forces the volume to dismount before the scan is performed.
/i	Performs a less vigorous check of index entries.
/c	Skips checking of cycles within the folder structure.
/v	Use /v to display a list of every file on a FAT or FAT32 volume; it has no meaning on an NTFS disk.

Clipbook Viewer   \windows\system32\clipbrd.exe

The Clipbook Viewer is provided as a "window" into the clip-board, so to speak, as it allows you to view whatever has been placed in the clipboard without disrupting or interfering with it any way. You can also save and retrieve clipboard data and share data with other users on your network.

Command Prompt   \windows\system32\cmd.exe

Start → All Programs → Accessories → Command Prompt

The command prompt is a simple application in which you type commands rather than pointing and clicking. It provides access to programs and utilities otherwise inaccessible and even permits the use of some advanced file management functions. Part VI fully documents the command prompt and supported commands. Cmd accepts the following parameters:

```
cmd [/q][/d] [/a|/u] [/e:on|off][/f:on|off]
    [/v:on|off] /t:fg [[/s][/c|/k] string]
```

Option	Description
string	When used with /c or /k, specifies a command to be carried out when the command prompt is first opened. Multiple commands are separated by &&, and string, as a whole, is surrounded by quotation marks. String must be the last parameter on the command line.
/c	Carries out the command specified by string and then stops.
/k	Carries out the command specified by string and continues.
/s	Strips any quotation marks in string.
/q	Turns the echo off; see "Echo" in Part VI.

Option	Description
/d	Disables execution of AutoRun commands. Without /d, any programs or commands listed in the Registry keys, HKEY_LOCAL_MACHINE\Software\Microsoft\Command Processor\AutoRun and HKEY_CURRENT_USER\Software\Microsoft\Command Processor\AutoRun are executed every time a command prompt window is opened.
/a	Formats all output so that it is ANSI-compliant.
/u	Formats all output so that it is Unicode-compliant.
/e:on|off	Enables or disables command extensions (the default is on).
/f:on|off	Enables or disables file and directory name completion (the default is off).
/v:on|off	Enables or disables delayed environment variable expansion (the default is off).
/t:fg	Sets the foreground and background colors (f and g, respectively) of the command prompt window. The single-digit values for f and g are as follows: 0=Black, 1=Blue, 2=Green, 3=Aqua, 4=Red, 5=Purple, 6=Yellow, 7=White, 8=Gray, 9=Light blue, A=Light green, B=Light aqua, C=Light red, D=Light purple, E=Light yellow, and F=Bright white.

> **TIP** Also included with Windows XP is *command.com*, the command prompt used in Windows 9x/Me. It's used similarly to *cmd.exe*, but has limited support of long filenames and other XP features. *Command.com* is included for legacy purposes only, and should be avoided; *cmd.exe* is the preferred command prompt in Windows XP.

Control Panel
\windows\system32\control.exe

Start → Control Panel (when using new Windows XP Start Menu)
Start → Settings → Control Panel (when using classic Start Menu)

The Control Panel has no settings of its own; it's merely a container for any number of options windows (commonly called applets or Control Panel extensions), most of which can be accessed without even opening the Control Panel folder.

A new optional feature in Windows XP divides the contents of the Control Panel into discrete categories. Unfortunately, these categories appear only when Control Panel is viewed as a standalone window (you won't see them in the Start Menu or in Explorer) and end up making the Control Panel more difficult to use. If you have Explorer's "Show common tasks in folders" option turned on (Explorer → Tools → Folder Options → General tab), the first entry in the tasks pane (named either "Switch to Classic View" or "Switch to Category View") allows you to turn categories off or on, respectively.

Table 3 shows how individual Control Panel icons are categorized, and how they can be launched from the command line.

Table 3. Control Panel applets and how to get to them

Applet name	Category	Command line[a]
Accessibility Options	Accessibility Options	control access.cpl
Add Hardware	n/a	control hdwwiz.cpl
Add or Remove Programs	Add or Remove Programs	control appwiz.cpl
Administrative Tools	Performance and Maintenance	control admintools
Date and Time	Date, Time, Language, and Regional Options	control date/time
Display	Appearance and Themes	control desktop control color
Folder Options	Appearance and Themes	control folders
Fonts	n/a	control fonts
Game Controllers	Printers and Other Hardware	control joy.cpl
Internet Options	Network and Internet Connections	control inetcpl.cpl
Keyboard	Printers and Other Hardware	control keyboard
Mouse	Printers and Other Hardware	control mouse

Table 3. Control Panel applets and how to get to them (continued)

Applet name	Category	Command line[a]
Network Connections	Network and Internet Connections	control netconnections
Phone and Modem Options	Printers and Other Hardware	control telephony
Power Options	Performance and Maintenance	control powercfg.cpl
Printers and Faxes	Printers and Other Hardware	control printers
Regional and Language Options	Date, Time, Language, and Regional Options	control intl.cpl
Scanners and Cameras	Printers and Other Hardware	n/a
Scheduled Tasks	Performance and Maintenance	control schedtasks
Sounds and Audio Devices	Sounds, Speech, and Audio Devices	control mmsys.cpl
Speech	Sounds, Speech, and Audio Devices	control speech
System	Performance and Maintenance	control sysdm.cpl
Taskbar and Start Menu	Appearance and Themes	n/a
User Accounts	User Accounts	control userpasswords

a Those items with "n/a" can't be launched from the command line, but you can create shortcuts (by dragging and dropping), which can subsequently be launched from the command prompt.

Create Shared Folder   *\windows\system32\shrpubw.exe*

The easiest way to begin sharing a folder or drive is to right-click on its icon in Explorer, select Sharing and Security, and turn on the "Share this folder on the network" option. However, this procedure allows you to share only local folders. If you need to access an unshared folder on a remote computer and you have administrative rights on that machine, you can use the Create Shared Folder utility. To share resources on a remote computer, use the /s parameter, like this: shrpubw /s *computer_name*. Then, fill in the Folder to share field (the full *local* path of the folder), the

Share name (the name under which the folder will be known on the network), and the optional Share description.

Date and Time
\windows\system\timedate.cpl

Control Panel → [Date, Time, Language and Regional Options] → Date and Time

The Date and Time dialog is pretty straightforward. Set your system's clock with the Date & Time tab, and your time zone with the Time Zone tab. The Internet Time tab allows you to automatically synchronize your PC's clock with one of several Internet time servers; just make sure your time zone and daylight savings settings are set properly; otherwise, the time synchronization will set the wrong time.

Device Manager
\windows\system32\devmgmt.msc

Control Panel → [Performance and Maintenance] → System → Hardware tab → Device Manager

keyboard shortcut: ⊞ + Pause/Break

Device Manager is the central interface for gathering information about and making changes to all the hardware installed in a system. Expand the branches and right-click any device to access its properties, to enable or disable the device, to uninstall the device, or to update the driver.

Disk Cleanup
\windows\system32\cleanmgr.exe

Start → All Programs → Accessories → System Tools → Disk Cleanup

Disk Cleanup allows you to reclaim disk space by helping you remove unwanted files from your hard drive.

Disk Defragmenter
\windows\system32\dfrg.msc

Start → All Programs → Accessories → System Tools → Disk Defragmenter

Disk defragmenter reorganizes the files and folders on any drive so that not only are the files stored contiguously, but the free space is also contiguous. An optimized disk will yield better performance and reliability. Highlight a drive and click Defragment to begin the defragmentation process. Or click Analyze to view a fragmentation report and a recommendation; Disk Defragmenter will claim that defragmentation is unnecessary if the percentage of fragmented files in the drive is lower than about 3%.

> **TIP** You can run other programs while Disk Defragmenter runs in the background, but this is not recommended for several reasons. Not only will writing to the disk interfere with Disk Defragmenter, causing it to restart repeatedly, but defragmenting a drive can substantially slow system performance.

DiskPart
\windows\system32\diskpart.exe

DiskPart is a full-featured program used to prepare hard disks, and optionally divide them into two or more partitions. The Disk Management tool (*diskmgmt.msc*) is the Windows equivalent. Start DiskPart and then type help to view a list of all the available commands; some of the more useful commands follow:

Command	Description
active	Activates the current basic partition so that it can be used as a boot disk; not necessary if it's the only partition.
assign	Assign a drive letter or mount point to the selected volume. Note that it is usually easier to use the Disk Management tool to do this.
create	Create a volume or partition.
delete	Delete an object (undoes the create command).
detail	Display details about an disk, partition, or volume. Note that you'll need to use select, first.
exit	Exit DiskPart (Ctrl-C also works).
extend	Extend a volume to fill free space immediately thereafter.
list	Display a list of all disks, partitions, or volumes.
remove	Remove a drive letter or mount point assignment (undoes the assign command).
select	Choose a disk, partition, or volume to view or modify. Use list to obtain object numbers for use with select.

Each of these commands (with the exception of exit) has one or more subcommands. For example, type detail at the prompt to get a list of the subcommands for use with the list command: disk, partition, and volume. So, to display a list of all the disk volumes on the system, type list volume. To select a volume, type select volume 1. Subsequent commands will then apply to the currently selected volume.

Display Properties

Control Panel → [Appearance and Themes] → Display
right-click on an empty portion of your Desktop → Properties

The Display Properties window allows you to configure a wide variety of settings that affect the Desktop, display, and appearance of just about anything on the screen. See Part for a list of settings and where to find them.

DriverQuery   \windows\system32\driverquery.exe

Although Device Manager (see the Microsoft Management Console) displays a hierarchal view of all the devices attached to the system, only Driver Query (included in Windows XP Professional only) provides a comprehensive list for every installed driver, either on the local machine or any remote computer on the network. Run DriverQuery without any options to print out the basic list, or use one of the following options:

```
driverquery [/fo format] [/nh] [/si] [/v] [/s system
[/u user [/p password]]]
```

Option	Description
/fo format	Specify the format of the display: /fo table for a formatted table, /fo list, for a plaint text list, or /fo csv for a comma-separated report.
/nh	If using the /fo table or /fo csv format (above), the /nh option turns off the column headers.
/v	Displays additional details about unsigned drivers.
/si	Displays additional details about signed drivers.
/s system	Connect to a remote system.
/u user /p password	Specify a user account and password under which the command executes.

FAT to NTFS Conversion Utility

\windows\system32\convert.exe

The filesystem is the invisible mechanism on any drive that is responsible for keeping track of all the data stored on the drive. This tool converts a drive using the FAT (File Allocation Table) filesystem to the more robust NTFS (NT File System) without damaging the data stored on it. Among other things, NTFS provides much more sophisticated security than FAT or FAT32 (used in most previous versions of Windows), as well as encryption and compression. The syntax is as follows:

```
convert volume /fs:ntfs [/v] [/cvtarea:fn] [/nosecurity]
[/x]
```

To convert drive *c:*, for example, type convert c: /fs:ntfs. The following options are also available:

Option	Description
/v	Run the Conversion Utility in verbose mode (provides more information).
/cvtarea: *filename*	Specifies a file to be the place holder for NTFS files.
/nosecurity	Sets the initial security privileges for the drive such that all files and folders will be accessible by all users.
/x	Forces the volume to dismount, closing any opened files.

 TIP To determine the filesystem currently used on any drive, right-click the drive icon in Explorer and select Properties.

Fax Console

\windows\system32\fxsclnt.exe

Start → All Programs → Accessories → Communications → Fax → Fax Console

The Fax Console is the central interface for sending, receiving, and managing faxes using the Microsoft Fax service and your modem. Start the Fax Monitor (Tools → Fax Monitor) to automatically answer incoming calls and receive faxes; to receive a single fax without automatically answering all calls, go to File → Receive a fax now.

There are two ways to send a fax using this service. The first, using File → Send a Fax (which is the same as running *fxssemd.exe* or selecting Start → All Programs → Accessories → Communications → Fax → Send a Fax), walks you through selecting a document and then creating a corresponding fax job. The preferred method of sending a fax, though, is to start the application used to create the original document and print to your fax printer. After your application has sent the document to the fax printer driver, a new Wizard appears and asks you for the recipient name and phone number, as well as any queuing options.

Fax Cover Page Editor   *\windows\system32\fxscover.exe*

Start → All Programs → Accessories → Communications → Fax → Fax Cover Page Editor

Fax Console → Tools → Personal Cover Pages → New (or) Open

Pages created with the Cover Page Editor are used automatically when sending faxes with the Microsoft Fax service. The Fax Cover Page Editor works like an ordinary drawing/layout program, in that you can indiscriminately place text, shapes, and images on a blank page. Next, use the Insert menu to place text fields on the page, into which the details of the fax will be placed when it is sent.

When you've created or modified the cover pages desired, save each into a Cover Page (*.cov*) file, stored, by default, in *\Documents and Settings\[username]\My Documents\Fax\Personal Coverpages*. And then, when sending a fax, simply specify the desired Cover Page file, and it will be used as the first page in your outgoing fax.

File Compare (comp)   *\windows\system32\comp.exe*

File Compare (*comp.exe*) compares two files (or more, using wild-cards), and reports whether the files are identical; if they are, you'll see Files compare OK. If the files are the same size but have different contents, *comp.exe* displays the differences, character by character, by reporting Compare Error at OFFSET *n* (where *n* is byte offset—the location of the difference, in characters, from the beginning of the file). If the files are different sizes, *comp.exe* reports Files are different sizes, and the comparison stops there. Here are the options for *comp.exe*:

```
comp [file1] [file2] [/n=number] [/c] [/off] [/d] [/l]
```

Option	Description
file1, file2	Specify the filenames of the files to compare.
/n=*number*	Compare only a few lines; example: /n=5
/c	Treat upper- and lowercase letters as identical.
/off	Include offline files; see the Synchronization Manager.
/d	Displays differences in decimal format.
/l	Include line numbers in the output.

TIP *Comp.exe* will ask if you want to perform another comparison, unless you use the input redirection character (see Part VI), like this:

```
comp file1 file2 <n
```

File Compare (fc)

\windows\system32\fc.exe

File Compare (*fc.exe*) compares the contents of two files (or more, using wildcards), and displays the differences (if any). If the files are identical, *fc.exe* will report FC: no differences encountered. If the files are different, *fc.exe* lists the differing lines. To compare two files, type fc bill.txt marty.txt. The output will look something like this:

```
Comparing files Bill.txt and Marty.txt
***** Bill.txt
Way down Louisiana close to New Orleans
Way back up in the woods among the evergreens
There stood a log cabin made of earth and wood
***** Marty.txt
Way down Louisiana close to New Orleans
Way back up in the woods among the antihistamines
There stood a log cabin made of earth and wood
*****
```

For each line or sequence of lines that is found to differ in the two files, *fc.exe* prints out a pair of excerpts from each file. The first and last line in each excerpt are what the two files have in common, and are included for context. The lines in between (only a single line in this example) show the differences. The syntax for *fc.exe* is as follows:

```
fc file1 file2 [/a] [/b] [/c] [/lbn] [/n] [/t] [/w] [/off]
[/nnn]
```

The options *file1*, *file2*, */c*, and */off* and are the same as those for File Compare (comp), discussed previously.

Option	Description
/a	Display only first and last lines for each set of differences, as opposed to the default of every different line.
/b	Treat the files as binary and perform the comparison on a byte-by-byte basis. Instead of the pairs of excerpts explained above, differing bytes are displayed in parallel columns. Unlike *comp.exe*, the other file comparison utility, the comparison will still be performed if they are different sizes. The /b option can't be used in conjunction with any of the other options.
/lbn	Limit the number of mismatches found to *n* (default is 100).
/n	Include line numbers in the report.
/t	Preserve any tabs in the files being compared.
/w	Compress tabs and spaces to a single space for comparison.
/nnn	Specify the number of consecutive lines that must match after a mismatch. For example, if you type /4, a mismatched line followed by 3 matching lines followed by one or more mismatched lines is treated as though it were a single sequence of mismatched lines.
/u	Treat the files as unicode text.

File and Settings Transfer Wizard \windows\system32\usmt\migwiz.exe

Start → All Programs → Accessories → System Tools → File and Settings Transfer Wizard

The File and Settings Transfer Wizard is a step-by-step guide that helps you transfer your personal documents, contents of your Favorites folder, Internet Explorer and Outlook Express settings, Desktop and display preferences, dial-up connections, and other Windows settings from one computer to another.

Folder Options

Control Panel → [Appearance and Themes] → Folder Options
Windows Explorer → Tools → Folder Options

The Folder Options contains settings that affect Windows Explorer, and how folder windows and file listings look and behave. See Part   for a list of all Windows settings. Some of the more confusing Folder Options are documented here:

Setting	Description
Common Tasks	The common tasks pane appears along the left side of folder listings in Explorer and single-folder windows, which contains information and links related to the currently selected folder and file. Of note is the feature to turn on or off the category view in Control Panel, a setting unavailable if the common tasks pane is disabled.
Display the simple folder view in Explorer's Folders list	This option simply shows or hides the dotted lines shown in the collapsible folder tree in Windows Explorer.
Display the contents of system folders	Enable this option to eliminate the warning that appears when you open certain folders, such as *c:* and *\Windows*.
Hide extensions for known file types	See below for reasons why this option should always be turned off.
Launch folder windows in a separate process	This starts a new instance of the Windows Explorer application every time you open a new folder window; although it consumes slightly more memory, it means that if one Explorer window crashes, they won't all crash.
Use Simple File Sharing	Despite the "Recommended" note here, it is strongly recommended that this option be disabled for security purposes.

About file types

The term *file types* describes the collection of associations between documents and the applications that use them. For example, Windows knows to run Notepad when you double-click on a file with the *.txt* extension (such as *Readme.txt*).

> **TIP**   By default, Windows hides the extensions of regis-
> tered file types in Explorer and on the Desktop, but
> it's best to have them displayed (set in the View tab).
> File extensions allow you to easily determine what
> kind of file you're dealing with (because icons are al-
> most never descriptive enough). They also allow you
> to change how Windows interacts with a file by sim-
> ply renaming the extension.

All registered file extensions and their descriptions are shown in the Registered file types list. Select any file type from the list and click Advanced.

The Actions listbox that appears contains a list of the customizable context menu items. The bold item is the default action, also shown in bold at the top of the context menu. Each entry has a name and a command line; a typical command line (the one for the *.txt* file type) might look like this: notepad /p "%1". This instructs Windows to launch Notepad with the /p parameter when you double-click on a *.txt* file. The %1 signifies the name of the selected file, and the quotation marks ensure compatiblity with any spaces in the filenames.

Fonts Folder

The *Fonts* folder is merely a folder on your hard disk (specifically, *\Windows\Fonts*). However, when viewed in Explorer, it's configured to display a list of installed fonts instead of a list of the contents of the folder.

TIP   Select View → Details for the most useful listing, which among other things, allows you to match up a font name with the file in which it's stored.

To view a preview of an installed font, just double-click its name. To delete a font, just delete it as you would any file (press the Delete key or drag-drop it into the Recycle Bin). To install a font (as long as it's one of the supported types), just drag-drop it into the *Fonts* folder. Supported typeface formats include TrueType (*.ttf*), Adobe Type 1 (*.pfm* and *.pfb*), OpenType (also known as TrueType v2), and ugly old raster fonts (*.fon*) used in early versions of Windows.

Format
\windows\system32\format.com

Before data can be stored on a floppy disk, hard disk, or any of a variety of removable media disks (such as Zip disks), the disk must be formatted. This process creates various low-level data structures on the disk, such as the filesystem (FAT, FAT32, NTFS, etc.). It also tests the disk surface for errors and stores bad sectors in a table that will keep them from being used. If there's any data on the disk, it will be erased. The options for Format are:

```
format volume [/q] [/c] [/x] [/v:label] [/fs:filesystem]
```

Option	Description
volume	The drive letter, followed by a colon, containing the media to be formatted. Example: format a:.
/q	Performs a "quick" format (only wipes out the file table).
/c	Compress all files by default (NTFS volumes only).
/x	Forces the volume to dismount first if necessary.
/v:label	Specifies the volume label, an arbitrary title you assign to any disk. It can be up to 11 characters and can include spaces.
/fs:filesystem	Specifies the filesystem; can be fat, fat32, or ntfs.

Freecell

\windows\system32\freecell.exe

Start → All Programs → Games → FreeCell

Freecell is a solitaire card game, the object of which is to move all the cards to the home cells. Like Klondike (see "Solitaire"), cards are rearranged by placing cards of descending value and alternating color (the 4 of clubs can be placed on the 5 of hearts or the 5 of diamonds). Click a card to highlight it and click another card to move the highlighted card. Cards can also be moved to one of the four "free cells," temporary storage slots, which fill up fast.

FTP

\windows\system32\ftp.exe

FTP (File Transfer Protocol) is used to transfer files to and from a remote computer, typically over an Internet connection. When you start FTP, you are connecting to a remote host, to which commands are issued by typing in the prompt. (If you specify an *ftp://* URL, the commands are typed automatically.)

Command	Description
ascii	Sets the file transfer type to ASCII (plain text), useful if you're transferring text files between Unix and Windows systems. Such translation will corrupt binary files, though, so you should use the binary command if you're not transferring ASCII files.
binary	Sets the file transfer type to binary, a crucial step for transferring nontext files (such as *.zip*, *.gif*, and *.doc*) between Unix and Windows-based machines. See also: ascii.
bye	Disconnects and ends the FTP session.
cd *remote_folder*	Changes the working directory on the remote computer (to cd on the local machine, use lcd).
delete *remote_file*	Deletes a single file on the remote computer. To delete multiple files with wildcards (see Part VI), use mdelete instead.
dir	Displays a list of the contents of the working directory on the remote computer, with details. See dir in Part VI.
get *remote_file* [*local_file*]	Transfers *remote_file* from the server to the local machine, optionally renaming it to *local_file*. If transferring binary (nontext) files, use the binary command first. To transfer multiple files with wildcards, use mget instead.
lcd [*directory*]	Changes the working directory on the *local* computer.
mkdir *directory*	Creates a remote directory; see mkdir in Part VI.
prompt	Turns on or off prompting for multiple file transfers (mput, mget, etc.)
put *local_file* [*remote_file*]	Transfers *local_file* from the server to the local machine, optionally renaming it to *remote_file*. If transferring binary (nontext) files, use the binary command first. To transfer multiple files with wildcards, use mput instead.
rmdir *remote_directory*	Deletes a remote directory.

Game Controllers

Control Panel → [Printers and Other Hardware] → Game Controllers

Before a joystick or other game controller can be used with Windows-based games, its driver must be installed in the Game Controllers dialog. If your game controller doesn't appear in this list, click Add. If your device doesn't show up on the list, and the manufacturer doesn't provide native Windows XP drivers, try Custom to set up a rudimentary configuration for the device.

Hearts   \windows\system32\mshearts.exe

Start → All Programs → Games → Hearts

Hearts is a trick-based game, like Spades or Wizard™, but the object is to have the lowest score at the end of each hand. One player puts down a card, and all other players must follow suit; if a player doesn't have a card of the matching suit, any card can be played. The highest card played takes all cards; there is no "trump" suit. Each heart is worth one point, the queen of spades is worth 13 points, and the jack of diamonds is worth −10 points; all other cards have no value.

Normally, the object of Hearts is to stick your opponents with as many points (hearts) as possible. However, if one player takes all the points in a hand, it's called *shooting the moon*; that player gets zero points, and everyone else gets 26 points.

Internet Explorer   \program files\internet explorer\iexplore.exe

Start → All Programs → Internet Explorer
Use the the Internet Explorer icon on the Desktop or on the QuickLaunch toolbar

Internet Explorer (IE) is a full-featured web browser that can be used to navigate the Web, as well as view web content on your local network or hard drive. Web content typically consists of web pages (*.html*), but can also be images (*.gif* and *.jpg* files), FTP sites, or even streaming video or audio.

Navigation in IE is accomplished by clicking hyperlinks in web pages, or by typing addresses in IE's address bar. Frequently visited sites can be "bookmarked" by creating Internet Shortcuts (similar to Windows Shortcuts), stored in your Favorites folder, your Desktop, or anywhere else on your hard disk. Use the Back and Next buttons (Alt-left arrow and Alt-right arrow, respectively) to navigate through the history; use the Stop button (or press Esc) to stop the loading of a page, and use the Refresh button (or press F5) to reload the page.

TIP
Go to Tools → Windows Update to view and optionally download any updates to Windows XP. See "Windows Update" for details.

If IE is the default browser, you can also go to Start → Run and type any web address to open the pages that addressed in IE. However, any browser can be set as the default. Typically, during installation of another browser, such as Netscape (*http://www.netscape.com*), Mozilla (*http://www.mozilla.org*), or Opera (*http://www.opera.com*), there will be an option to make that browser the default.

Internet Options

Control Panel → [Network and Internet Connections] → Internet Options
Internet Explorer → Tools → Internet Options

The Internet Options dialog is a densly packed dialog with about every conceivable option for Internet Explorer. All these settings are listed by function in Part . Among the concepts used in this dialog are the following:

Temporary Internet Files (a.k.a. the browser cache)
> A folder on your hard disk that stores copies of recently visited web pages for quicker access the next time they're visited. By default, the Temporary Internet Files folder is located in *\Documents and Settings\[username]\Local Settings\ Temporary Internet Files*.

Cookies
> Pieces of information stored on your computer to allow certain web sites to remember your identity or preferences; click Delete Cookies to clear all cookies stored on your computer. To selectively remove cookies, open the *\Documents and Settings\[username]\Cookies* folder in Windows Explorer. See the Privacy tab for more Cookie settings.

Keyboard Properties

Control Panel → [Printers and Other Hardware] → Keyboard

The Keyboard Properties dialog controls the way characters are repeated when keys are held down, as well as how quickly the text cursor (insertion point) blinks. Tip: move the Repeat rate slider all the way to the right (towards Fast), and your computer will actually seem faster.

Logoff

\windows\system32\logoff.exe

Logoff is a quick way to log off the current user (either sitting in front of the computer or logged in remotely), rather than doing so through the Start Menu; you can even create a shortcut to allow you to quickly end the current session. The syntax is as follows:

```
logoff [session | id] [/server:name] [/v]
```

Option	Description
session | id	The name or ID of the session to end (never both).
/server:name	Specifies the remote terminal server (remote desktop) hosting the session to end.
/v	Displays additional information.

Microsoft Chat

\windows\system32\winchat.exe

Microsoft Chat is a simple chat program that allows two users to have a text-based conversation using two computers connected over a network. The screen is split in two panes, in which each user types and watches as the other types. Both screens are updated in real time, so you can see the letters as they're typed by your partner. Click the Dial button to initiate a chat session.

Microsoft Magnifier

\windows\system32\magnify.exe

Start → All Programs → Accessories → Accessibility → Magnifier

The Microsoft Magnifier is used to assist those with visual impairments by magnifying a portion of the screen. When you start Magnifier, the top 15% of the screen turns into an automatic magnifying glass, which follows the mouse cursor around the screen. The Magnifier can be resized or moved with the mouse.

Microsoft Management Console   \windows\system32\mmc.exe

Start → All Programs → Administrative Tools → Computer Management

The Microsoft Management Console (MMC) is a host for many of the administrative tools that come with Windows XP. Each tool that works with MMC is called a "Snap-in." Several Snap-ins can be shown in MMC at any given time and appear as entries in the Explorer-style tree in the left pane.

A collection of one or more Snap-ins can be saved into a Console (*.msc*) file, which is a small file that simply lists Snap-ins to display in the Console window. More than a dozen predefined Console files are included with Windows, and you can modify them (or even create your own) by adding or removing Snap-ins or creating custom "Taskpad Views," pages with lists of shortcuts to programs or other Snap-ins.

> **TIP**   To add a Snap-in to the current Console file (select File → New to start a new Console), go to File → Add/Remove Snap-in, and click Add. Then, choose one of the available Snap-ins (note that not all Snap-ins described here are available in all versions of Windows XP), and click Add to add it to the list in the previous window. MMC allows you to use most of these tools on remote systems; for example, you can run Device Manager on a machine in another office. Most Snap-ins will prompt you for a remote computer name when you first add them to the current console.

Snap-in	.msc file	Description
ActiveX Control	*n/a*	Use this Snap-in to add an ActiveX control to your console file.
Certificates	*certmgr.msc*	Browse all the security certificates used by Internet Explorer and IIS (Windows XP Professional only).

Snap-in	.msc file	Description
Component Services	*comexp.msc*	Manage installed COM (component object model) components.
Computer Management	*compmgmt.msc*	A collection of 13 other Snap-ins.
Device Manager	*devmgmt.msc*	See "Device Manager," earlier in this chapter.
Disk Defragmenter	*drfg.msc*	See "Disk Defragmenter," earlier in this chapter.
Disk Management	*diskmgmt.msc*	The Disk Management Snap-in lists all installed drives, including hard disks, CD drives, and other removable storage devices (except floppies). Here, you can change drive letters, create or delete partitions (see also "DiskPart").
Event Viewer	*eventvwr.msc*	View the three system event logs: Application, Security, and System. The Application log lists every application crash, status report, and warning generated by services. The Security log records events such as valid and invalid logon attempts, as well as events related to the use of shared resources. The system log contains events logged by Windows XP system components, such as driver failures and system startup errors.
Folder		Organize Snap-ins in the tree display.
FrontPage Server Extensions		Manage the various extensions to FrontPage Server and any corresponding settings.
Group Policy (Local Computer Policy)	*gpedit.msc*	A collection of policy settings, controlling startup and shutdown scripts, security settings for Internet Explorer, and user account policies.
Indexing Service	*ciadv.msc*	Collects information from the documents on your hard disk, and compiles a database used to enhance searches. The Indexing Service indexes *.html* files, *.txt* files, Microsoft Office documents, Internet mail and news, and any other document for which a document filter is available. The Indexing Service Snap-in allows you to manage the directories that are routinely scanned and query the database catalog.

Snap-in	.msc file	Description
Internet Information Services	*iis.msc*	Administers the various functions associated with the Web/FTP/SMTP server service. For example, you can configure how CGI scripts are running from web pages posted on the server.
IP Security Monitor		Monitor IP Security status; see IP Security Policy Management.
IP Security Policy Management		Manage IPSec (Internet Protocol Security) policies for secure communication with other computers.
Link to Web Address		Include a link to a software downloads site, an HTTP-based administration web page, or another troubleshooting site, such as *http://www. annoyances.org*.
Local Users and Groups	*lusrmgr.msc*	Provides more advanced settings, using a simpler and more direct interface, then Control Panel → User Accounts. You can set password expiration, assign users to groups, manage logon scripts, change the location of a user's home folder, and other advanced options.
Performance Logs and Alerts	*perfmon.msc*	Collect performance data automatically from certain applications, and then create logs that can be exported then analyzed. The applications designed to generate performance logs are typically associated with web servers.
Removable Storage Management	*ntmsmgr.msc*	View all the devices that support removable media, such as CD and DVD drives, CD and DVD writers, tape drives, Zip drives, flash memory readers, and other such devices. This tool labels, catalogs, and tracks media, and stores this information into libraries. Media Pools, collections of removable media to have the same management policies, are used to organize these libraries.
Resultant Set of Policy	*rsop.msc*	Allows you to view and change the policy settings for a particular user.
Security Configuration and Analysis		Used to view and manage security databases for computers using Security Templates (see next entry), and is especially helpful for tracking changes to security.
Security Templates	*secpol.msc*	Used to create security policies.

Snap-in	.msc file	Description
Services	services.msc	A service is a program that runs invisibly in the background, usually started when Windows starts, but before any user logs in. Windows XP comes with nearly 80 services preinstalled, some of which may be active (started). Double-click any service in the list to view its properties, such as its status (Started or Stopped), whether it's started automatically, under which user accounts it is enabled, what actions to take if the service encounters a problem, and which other components the service depends on (if any).
Shared Folders	fsmmgmt.msc	Lists all the resources shared over the network.
WMI Control	wmimgmt.msc	WMI (Windows Management Instrumentation) is set of standards for accessing and sharing management information over an enterprise network.

Microsoft NetMeeting   \program files\netmeeting\conf.exe

Start → All Programs → Accessories → Communications → NetMeeting

NetMeeting allows videoconferencing (videophone) and voice conferencing over a network or Internet connection. The connection is made via either a central directory service (Microsoft provides several), or directly to another user's IP address. To initiate a voice conference (audio only), you'll need an Internet connection and a sound card, speakers, and a microphone on each end. For video conferencing, you'll also need a videoconferencing camera and a high-speed connection.

To start a conference, type the recipient's email address or IP address into the text field at the top of the window, and press enter or click the little telephone button. If recipient is also running NetMeeting, it will "ring" when a call is received. Hang up any call by clicking the Hang Up button or by going to Call → Hang Up.

Minesweeper   \windows\system32\winmine.exe

Start → All Programs → Games → Minesweeper

The object of Minesweeper is to uncover "safe" areas on a playing field without hitting on any landmines. Click any square with the left mouse button to uncover it; if it's a mine, the game is over. Otherwise, you'll either see a number, corresponding to the number of mines immediately adjacent to the clicked square, or the square will be blank, meaning that there are no adjacent mines. Use the numbers as hints to where the mines are located; use the process of elimination to uncover all the squares that aren't mines. Use the right mouse button to mark uncertain squares and protect them from being accidentally clicked.

Mouse Properties

Control Panel → [Printers and Other Hardware] → Mouse

The Mouse Properties dialog controls the buttons and motion of your pointing device, and the appearance of the various mouse cursors, such as the arrow and hourglass.

 TIP It's a good idea to save your custom pointer selections in a "Scheme" (under the Pointers tab), since any changes to the "Theme" selection in Display Properties will revert all pointers to their defaults.

Msg

\windows\system32\msg.exe

Msg is used to send a text message to a single user or all currently logged-on users on any computer on your network. The message will appear as a pop-up message box. Msg accepts the following options:

```
msg recipient [/server:name] [/time:sec] [/v] [/w]
[message]
```

Option	Description
message	The text message to send.
recipient	The username, session name, session ID, or filename to receive the message. Specify an asterisk (*) to send a message to all sessions on the specified server.
/server:*name*	Specify /server:*name* to send the message to users on another machine, where *name* is the name of a Terminal Server.
/time:*sec*	Indicates the amount of time, in seconds, to wait for the recipient to acknowledge the message being sent.

Option	Description
/v	Verbose mode; displays additional information.
/w	Wait for a response from the recipient, useful with /v.

Narrator
\windows\system32\narrator.exe

Start → All Programs → Accessories → Accessibility → Magnifier

The Narrator is used to assist those with visual impairments by using a voice synthesizer and your computer's sound hardware to read aloud text and the titles of screen elements. Check the "Announced events on screen" option to have Narrator speak messages that appear, the titles of Windows when they are activated, and the captions of many types of screen elements. Narrator can also speak each letter and number as its corresponding key is pressed on the keyboard.

> **TIP** To read an entire window, click the window and then press Ctrl-Shift-Spacebar. To read the caption of the control with the focus, or to read the contents of a text field, press Ctrl-Shift-Enter. To get a more detailed description of an item, press Ctrl-Shift-Insert. To read the title bar of a window, press Alt-Home. To read the status bar of a window, press Alt-End. To silence the speech, press the Ctrl key by itself.

Network Connections
\windows\system\ncpa.cpl

Control Panel → [Network and Internet Connections] → Network Connections
Start → Settings → Network Connections (Classic Start Menu only)

The Network Connections folder is used to connect your computer to the Internet, to another computer on a local area network, and to other types of network resources.

A connection icon will automatically appear here for each network adapter installed in the system, but dial-up connections, VPN connections, and PPPoE connections must be added manually with the New Connection Wizard. Double-click any connection icon to view its connected status, or right-click any connection icon and select Properties to modify the connection.

Useful settings in a connection's Properties sheet include the TCP/IP settings, IP address, username and password (for dial-up, VPN, and PPPoE connections), and settings related to Internet Connection Sharing and the Internet Connection Firewall feature.

Network Setup Wizard

My Network Places → Network Setup Wizard
Start → All Programs → Accessories → Communications → Network Setup Wizard

The Network Setup Wizard walks you through some basic networking settings, and is intended to make it easy to set up Windows to work with your Internet connection or to gain access to other computers on your network. The first page of the Network Setup Wizard implies that the wizard will set up a network for you, help you set up Internet connection sharing, install a firewall, and share files and printers. In fact, it will do none of these things; rather, it will simply ensure that some of the necessary protocols are installed and properly configured for the type of network to which you plan on attaching your computer. Just follow the prompts and answer the questions the best you can. If the Network Setup Wizard prompts you to create a setup disk for use on other computers, answer "Just finish the wizard," as the disk is of little use. The Network Setup Wizard won't help you set up an Internet connection, but the "New Connection Wizard" will.

New Connection Wizard

\Program Files\Internet Explorer
Connection Wizard\icwconn1.exe

Control Panel → [Network and Internet Connections] → Network Connections → New
  Connection Wizard (or "Create a new connection")
Start → All Programs → Accessories → Communications → Connection Wizard

The New Connection Wizard will guide you through the process of setting up a new connection; the following four types, presented on the first page of the wizard, are available:

Option	Description
Connect to the Internet	Use this option to set up a new Internet connection; on the next page, choose "Set up my connection manually."

Option	Description
Connect to the network at my workplace	This option helps set up a remote connection to a business network, either through a dialup connection or through VPN (Virtual Private Networking), assuming your business network is set up to accept such connections.
Set up a home or small office network	Choose this option to run the Network Setup Wizard.
Set up an advanced connection	This last option is used to set up other types of connections, such as those that use a single serial or parallel cable (also known as "Direct Cable Connection") or those that communicate wirelessly with an infrared port. Note that the other computer involved must be first set up to "accept incoming connections" before you can connect to it.

TIP   There's no way to add a standard Ethernet connection with the New Connection Wizard. However, such connections will be automatically added for each network interface card detected in your computer. If an icon for your card does not appear, its drivers have not been properly installed.

Notepad

\windows\notepad.exe

Start → Program → Accessories → Notepad

Notepad is a rudimentary text editor that allows you to view and modify *.txt* files (plain text files), *.reg* files (Registry patch files), *.bat* files (batch files), *.ini* files (configuration files), *.html* files (web pages), and any other ASCII text-based file type.

TIP   Notepad has no intrinsic formatting of its own, so any file that is opened in Notepad is displayed exactly as it is stored on the hard disk, with the proviso that only visible characters will be shown. Although binary files will look like gibberish, there are times when opening them in Notepad can be useful. For example, if you suspect that an image file or a movie file has the wrong filename extension, you can open it in Notepad to look for markers near the beginning of the file to help identify its format.

The Word Wrap feature (Edit → Word Wrap) will break apart long lines of text so that they are visible in the Notepad window without horizontal scrolling. However, no permanent changes will be made to the file, so you can use the Word Wrap feature without fear of damaging the integrity of the document.

NSLookup

\windows\system32\nslookup.exe

NSLookup is a simple tool that allows you to look up the IP address of any domain name or server name, as well as find the server name associated with any particular IP address. If a connection to the Internet has been established, just open a command prompt window and type `nslookup servername` or `nslookup ip_address`. For example, if you type `nslookup 209.204.146.22`, you'll see that it corresponds to *www.oreilly.com*.

NTFS Compression Utility

\windows\system32\compact.exe

This tool allows you to view or configure the automatic file compression on NTFS drives from the command prompt. This feature can be more easily accessed by right-clicking on a file or folder, selecting Properties, clicking Advanced, and then turning on the "Compress contents to save disk space" option.

If you run the NTFS Compression Utility without any options, it will display the compression settings for the current directory and all its contents. The NTFS Compression Utility takes the following options:

```
compact [/c | /u] [/s[:dir]] [/a] [/i] [/f] [/q]
[filename]
```

Opt	Description
filename	Specifies a file, folder, or group of files (using wildcards; see Part VI).
/c	Compresses the specified file(s) or mark the specified folder(s) such that any files added will be automatically compressed.
/u	Uncompresses the specified file(s); opposite of /c.
/s	If a folder is specified for filename, the /c and /u parameters will act only on new files added to the folder. Include the /s parameter as well to compress or uncompress files already in the folder. If filename is omitted, use the /s option to act on all files in the current folder.

Opt	Description
/a	Includes files with hidden or system attributes set.
/i	Ignores errors.
/f	Forces compression on all already-compressed files.
/q	Quiet mode; report only the most essential information.

NTFS Encryption Utility

\windows\system32\cipher.exe

NTFS Encryption runs invisibly in the background, and is used to prevent unauthorized access to your data by other users on your system or network. Cipher, included only with Windows XP Professional, allows you to view or configure the automatic file encryption on NTFS drives from the command prompt. Most of the features of this tool can be more easily accessed by right-clicking on a file or folder, selecting Properties, clicking Advanced, and then turning on the "Encrypt contents to secure data" option.

If you run the NTFS Encryption Utility without any options, it will display the encryption settings for the current directory and all its contents. Otherwise, specify any of the following options:

```
cipher [/e|/d] [/s] [/a] [/i] [/f] [/q] [/h] [filename]
cipher [ /k | /r:efs_file | /w:dir | /u [/n]]
```

Option	Description
filename	Specifies a file, folder, or group of files (using wildcards; see Part VI).
/e	Encrypts the specified file(s) or marks the specified folder(s) such that any files added will be automatically encrypted.
/d	Decrypts the specified file(s); opposite of /e.
/s	Encrypts all subfolders of the specified folder(s).
/a	Operates on folders and all the files contained therein.
/i	Ignores errors.
/f	Forces encryption on already-encrypted files.
/q	Quiet mode; report only the most essential information.
/h	Includes files with hidden or system attributes set.
/k	Generates and displays a new file encryption key for the current user; not valid with any other options.

Option	Description
/r:efs_file	Generates an EFS (Encrypting File System) recovery agent key and certificate, then writes them to *efs_file.pfx* (containing the certificate and private key) and *efs_file.cer* file (containing only the certificate).
/w:dir	"Wipes" the drive containing directory *dir*, preventing subsequent recovery of any files with an "undelete" utility.
/u	Updates all encrypted files on all local drives to ensure that your file encryption key or recovery agent key are current; not valid with any other options except /n.
/n	Lists encrypted files without modifying them; type cipher /u /n to list all the encrypted files on your system.

> **TIP**
>
> Go to Control Panel → [Appearance and Themes] → Folder Options → View tab and turn on the "Show encrypted or compressed NTFS files in color" option to visually differentiate such files from unencrypted, uncompressed files.

On-Screen Keyboard
\windows\system32\osk.exe

Start → All Programs → Accessories → Accessibility → On-Screen Keyboard

Intended to be used by those who are unable to comfortably use a keyboard, the On-Screen Keyboard allows any key normally available on the keyboard to be pressed with click of the mouse or other pointing device.

You can click keys when another application has the focus. For example, open the On-Screen Keyboard, and then open your word processor; the keyboard will float above the word processor, allowing you to click any key to "type" it into your document.

Outlook Express
\program files\outlook express\msimn.exe

Start → All Programs → Outlook Express
Quick Launch Bar → "Launch Outlook Express"

Outlook Express is the email client included with Windows XP. Outlook Express uses an Explorer-like tree interface to manage the folders into which email messages are organized. Newly received messages are stored in the Inbox folder; files queued to be sent are stored in the Outbox folder, and then are moved to the Sent Items folder when they have been sent. The Deleted Items folder is like the Recycle Bin in that it stores deleted messages until it is manually emptied. And the Drafts folder stores messages as they're being composed. To add a new folder, select Local Folders in the tree, and then go to File → New → Folder. Messages can be moved from folder to folder by dragging and dropping. Here are some of the more interesting or confusing features of Outlook Express:

Accounts (Tools → Accounts)

Among other things, this dialog allows you to retreive email from more than one account. The "default" account will be used as your return address when sending outgoing email unless you change it on a per-message basis.

Identity Management (File → Identities → Manage Identities)

Identities allow more than one person use Outlook Express on the same machine. Each identity has its own set of accounts, settings, and mail. It's tempting to use Identities if you want to send out mail using more than one persona, but this really isn't what the feature is designed for. Instead, you should set up multiple accounts (see above), one for each "persona" you wish to assume.

To add a new identity, go to File → Identities → Add New Identity. You can then enter the name of the new user and select a password if needed. To switch identities at any time, select File → Switch Identity. To share contacts in your Address Book between identities, open the Address Book, select View → Folders and groups, and move (or copy) them into the Shared Contacts folder.

File Attachments (Insert → File Attachment)

This allows you to send a file along with an email message, typically better than attempting to "embed" files in messages. If Outlook Express is your default email program, you can also send a file as an email attachment by right-clicking it, and selecting Send To → Mail Recipient; this also works for any third-party email programs set as the default in Control Panel → Internet Options → Programs tab.

Options (Tools → Options)

Specify options that govern the behavior of Outlook Express, such as how often Outlook Express checks for mail and whether it is the default email program.

Message Rules (Tools → Message Rules)

Outlook Express can be set up to automatically handle incoming mail in a number of different ways: you can set up rules to store all email retrieved from your business account in a certain folder, all email retrieved from your personal account in a different folder, and all junk mail (spam) in the trash. Furthermore, you can have Outlook Express automatically respond to certain messages, mark some messages as urgent, and others as potentially annoying.

Conversations (Message → Watch Conversation, Message → Ignore Conversation)

A conversation is a continuous series of email or newsgroup messages, often called a thread. For example if you were to write an email with the subject, "Propane Elaine," it might spark a series of messages between you and the recipient, all of which would have the subject, "Re: Propane Elaine." This thread of messages is called a "conversation" in Outlook Express, and such threads can be "watched" so that special icons are placed next to the messages. Furthermore, if you select View → Current View → Group Messages by Conversation, messages in conversations will be grouped in expandable branches, like the folders in Explorer.

Signatures (Tools → Options → Signature tab)

A signature is a bit of text that is automatically placed at the end of every outgoing message you write. Turn on the "Add signatures to all outgoing messages" option, or go to Insert → Signature in the message composition window to use a signature on a per-message basis.

Stationary (Tools → Options → Compose tab)

Stationery is just as you expect; it imposes a visual style on your message, including colors and even images. Stationary files are just *.html* files (web pages), stored by default in *\Program Files\ Common Files\Microsoft Shared\Stationary*, and can be edited with any web page editor or plain text editor.

Paint

\windows\system32\mspaint.exe

Start → All Programs → Accessories → Paint

Paint is a basic image editor (often called a "paint program"), capable of creating and modifying most *.bmp*, *.jpg*, *.gif*, *.tif*, and *.png* image files.

At the bottom of the window, you'll see a color palette; the leftmost box shows the currently selected foreground and background colors. To the left of the document area is a simple toolbox. Each tool has a different function used to manipulate the image in some way, the use of which should be fairly self-evident.

Phone and Modem Options

\windows\system\telephon.cpl

Control Panel → [Printers and Other Hardware] → Phone and Modem Options

Used to connect to the Internet (unless you have DSL or a cable modem) and send and receive faxes, your modem is configured in this Control Panel dialog. The modems listed here are the same as those listed in the Modems branch in Device Manager, so if your modem doesn't appear, its driver has not been properly installed.

TIP

Dialing problems are often caused by improper dialing rules; make sure your area code and call waiting settings are correct. Multiple locations should be configured if you have a portable computer and need to dial out from within different area codes or from varying phone numbers with different dialing requirements.

Phone Dialer
\program files\windows nt\dialer.exe

Start → All Programs → Accessories → Communications → Phone Dialer

The primary Phone Dialer window is essentially a contact list, allowing you to initiate a telephone call, Internet call, or conference with one or more people.

To place a call, click the Dial button or select Phone → Dial; if no contact is selected (from either the Speed Dial folder or from one of the Internet Directories folders), you'll be prompted to enter the other party's contact info. A conference, as opposed to call, allows you to communicate with several users at once. To start a conference, click New in the toolbar, or go to Phone → New Conference. Then, other users call you to join the conference.

Pinball
\program files\windows nt\pinball\pinball.exe

Start → All Programs → Games → Pinball

Space Cadet 3D Pinball is a simple throwback to the classic pinball game. The ball is launched by holding the spacebar for a second or two to pull back the plunger, and letting go. By default, the left and right flippers are controlled with the Z and / keys, respectively. You can change the keys use play the game by going to Options → Player Controls.

Ping
\windows\system32\ping.exe

The primary function of Ping is to see if another computer is "alive" and reachable. Ping works on local networks and across Internet connections. For example, if you type ping oreilly.com at a command prompt and get at least one response like this:

```
Reply from 209.204.146.22: bytes=32 time=78ms TTL=238
```

it means that a successful connection was established and the remote system responded to the ping. Otherwise, you'll see Request timed out, meaning that it is down or the connection has been severed. The syntax of Ping is as follows:

```
ping target [-t] [-a] [-i ttl] [-n count] [-l size] [-f]
   [-w timeout] [-r count] [-s count] [-j host_list |
   -k host_list] [-v tos]
```

Option	Description
target	The name or IP address of the remote machine.
-a	Resolve IP addresses to hostnames.
-n *count*	Number of pings; default is 4. Has no meaning with -t.
-l *size*	The size of the packets to send, in bytes; default is 32 bytes.
-f	Turn on the "Don't Fragment" flag in packet.
-w *timeout*	The amount of time, in milliseconds, before Ping gives up and displays Request timed out; default is 500.
-r *count*	Display Tracert data, where count is the number of hops.
-s *count*	Display a time stamp for count hops.
-t	Pings continually until interrupted with Ctrl-C; press Ctrl-Break to show statistics without interrupting.
-j *host_list*	Impose a "loose" route (with -r) along which to ping.
-k *host_list*	Impose a "strict" route (with -r) along which to ping.
-i *ttl*	Specify the TTL (Time To Live); valid range 0 to 255.
-v *tos*	Specify the TOS (Type of Service); valid range 0 to 255.

Power Options

\windows\system\powercfg.cpl

Control Panel → [Performance and Maintenance] → Power Options

Advanced Power Management, primarily used to reduce power consumption or extend the life of your computer's battery, relies on cooperation between your computer's BIOS and operating system. Settings in this window allow you to choose how long Windows waits before your monitor, hard disk, and other devices are shut down, as well as when your computer hibernates or goes into "standby" mode. All power settings are listed in Part .

> **TIP**
> Before you mess with any settings here, make sure that APM support is enabled in your system BIOS, but all subordinate APM options are disabled or set to their minimum values. Refer to the documentation that came with your computer or motherboard, or see Appendix B of *Windows Annoyances* (O'Reilly).

Printers and Faxes

Start → Settings → Printers and Faxes (Classic Start Menu only)
Control Panel → [Printers and Other Hardware] → Printers and Faxes

The Printers and Faxes folder contains icons representing your installed printers and fax devices. Once a printer is installed here, you can print to it from within any application, drag documents to the its icon to print them, or double-click on the printer icon to see or change the status of current print jobs.

Right-click a printer icon and select Set as Default Printer to make that printer the default in all applications' print dialogs, or select Properties to change the default print settings for the printer. Double-click on any printer icon for a view of the printer's job queue. Finally, use the Add Printer wizard to install drivers for a local or network printer

Query Process   \windows\system32\qprocess.exe

Query Process is a simple command-line utility used to display a list of the running processes, programs running visibly in the foreground or invisibly in the background. Task Manager, which also does this, is easier to use, but less flexible. Query Process is used as follows:

```
qprocess [target] [/server:computer] [/system]
```

Option	Description
target	Specify a username to display the processes started by that user, or omit target to display all the processes started by the current user. Specify a session name or number (via /id:sessionid) to display all the processes started in that session. Specify a program name to display all the processes associated with that program. Specify * to list all processes.
/server: computer	Query a remote computer on your network.
/system	Include system processes.

Example

Type qprocess * /system to list all processes.

Regional and Language Options

\windows\system\intl.cpl

Control Panel → [Date, Time, Language, and Regional Options] → Regional and
Language Options

Numbers, times, dates, and currency are displayed differently in
different parts of the world, and the Regional and Language
Options dialog allows you to choose your display preferences in
painful detail, all of which are documented in Part .

Registry Console Utility

\windows\system32\reg.exe

The Registry Console Utility performs all the functions of the
Registry Editor, discussed in Part , but can be used from the
command line. It also does a few things Registy Editor can't do,
such as making a duplicate of a registry key or comparing two
registry keys. To use the Registry Console Utility, type reg followed
by one of the following commands and any applicable parameters:

Command	Description
query *keyname* [/v *valuename*	/ve] [/s]	Displays the data stored in a Registry value; omit /v *valuename* to display list of all the values in *keyname* (include /s to query all subkeys), or specify /ve to query the (Default) value. *Keyname* can also include the name of a remote computer, like this: query *computer\keyname*.
add *keyname* [/v *valuename*	/ve] [/d *data*] [/t *typ*] [/s *sep*] [/f]	Adds a new value. The *keyname*, *valuename*, /v, and /ve options are the same as with query, listed previously. The /d option assigns data to the new value; if omitted, the new value will be empty. Use /t to specify the data type for the value; the default is string (REG_SZ). Specify /f to overwrite existing values without prompting.
delete*keyname* [/v *valuename*	/ve	/va] [/f]	Deletes an existing value. All options are the same as with add, above. The /va parameter instructs the Registry Console Utility to delete all values in the specified key.
copy *keyname1 keyname2* [/s] [/f]	Duplicates a key and all its values, where *keyname1* is the full path of the source key, and *keyname2* is the full path of the new key. Specify /s to include all subkeys and their values, and use the /f option to skip the prompt.
save *keyname filename*	Saves a portion of the registry, *keyname*, into a binary hive file, *filename*. The root key in *keyname* must be a four-letter abbreviation (e.g., HKLM, HKCU, HKCR, HKU, HKCC). Use export to create a registry patch (*.reg*) file. See also restore.

Command	Description
restore *keyname* *filename*	Imports keyname from a hive file (created with save, listed previously) into the Registry. As with save, you must use the four-letter root key abbreviation.
load *keyname* *filename*	Mounts a hive file (created with save, above) onto the Registry. Load is similar to restore, above, except changes to the keys are subsequently written back to the source hive file.
unload *keyname*	Unmounts a key, *keyname*, that has been installed with load, above.
compare *keyname1* *keyname2* [/v *valuename* | /ve] [/s] [*output*]	Compares two keys or values, *keyname1* and *keyname2*. The /v, /ve, and /s options are the same as with add, listed earlier. Output can be /oa (output all differences and matches), /od (output only differences, the default), /os (output only matches), or /on (no output).
export *keyname* *filename*	Creates a registry patch (*.reg*), *filename*, from *keyname*. Registry patches can be imported with import, below, or by double-clicking in Explorer (via Registry Editor).
import *filename*	Imports a registry patch (*.reg*), *filename*, created either with export, listed earlier, or with the Registry Editor.

Registry Editor   *\windows\regedit.exe*

The Registry Editor provides a means to view and modify the contents of the Windows Registry, the master database that stores configuration settings for Windows XP and many of the applications on your computer. See Part for more information on the Registry and the use of Registry Editor.

Remote Assistance   *\windows\system32\rcimlby.exe -LaunchRA*

Start → All Programs → Remote Assistance

Remote Assistance works with several other Windows components to allow another user to connect to your computer using the Remote Desktop Connection.

The first step involves inviting another user to connect, which takes care of the very important step of transmitting your IP address and login information to the other user. You can send it either as an attachment via email, or via Windows Messenger. The remote user receives the invitation, double-clicks the attached file, and connects to your computer.

WARNING

Remote Assistance potentially allows unwanted access to your computer and data. Make sure to take advantage of the features in Remote Assistance to help protect your computer, such as requiring a password, and allowing remote connection only within the next hour. If you get the error, "Your current system settings prevent you from sending an invitation," it means that the Remote Assistance feature has been disabled for security reasons. You can reenable it by going to Control Panel → [Performance and Maintenance] → System → Remote tab, and turning on both of the options on this page.

Remote Copy

\windows\system32\rcp.exe

Remote Copy allows you to copy one or more files from one remote computer to another remote computer without first transferring the files to your own computer. Remote Copy takes the following parameters:

```
rcp [-b] [-h] [-r] source destination
```

Option	Description
source, destination	The full network path of the source file and destination, respectively. Note that wildcards (see Part VI) must be accompanied with an escape character: apple.* becomes apple.*
-b	Transfers the files with binary mode (see FTP)
-h	Transfers hidden files.
-r	Recursive; include subfolders when copying folders.

Examples

```
rcp -b \\cooder\c\docs\rings.txt \\spud\
rcp -b 192.168.0.1.cooder:c\docs\rings.txt 192.168.0.1.
spud:c\stuff
```

Remote Desktop Connection

\windows\system32\mstsc.exe

Start → All Programs → Accessories → Communications → Remote Desktop Connection

Remote Desktop Connection allows you to connect to another computer (or someone else to connect your computer) and use it as though you were sitting in front of it, complete with the Desktop and access to any Windows applications.

To configure a computer to accept incoming connections via Remote Desktop Connection, go to Control Panel → [Performance and Maintenance] → System → Remote tab, and turn on the "Allow users to connect remotely to this computer" option. See "Remote Assistance" for an easy way to transfer login information to another user.

Connect to a remote system by opening Remote Desktop Connection (Windows XP Professional only) and typing that computer's name (if connected on a local network) or that computer's IP address (if connected to the Internet).

Rundll32

\windows\system32\rundll32.exe

Rundll32 provides "string invocation," which lets you execute a command buried in a DLL (Dynamic Link Library) file from the command line or a Windows Shortcut. Rundll32 accepts the following options:

```
rundll32 filename,function_name [arguments... ]
```

Option	Description
filename	The filename of a DLL (.dll) file.
function_name	The case-sensitive name of a function in the DLL file.
function_arguments	Any parameters used by function_name; refer to the function's documentation for details. Note that any string parameters are case-sensitive.

Examples

```
rundll32 Rnaui.dll,RnaDial ConnectionName
rundll32 hnetwiz.dll,HomeNetWizardRunDll
rundll32 desk.cpl,InstallScreenSaver filename
rundll32 shimgvw.dll,ImageView_Fullscreen filename
```

Run As   \windows\system32\runas.exe

Use Run As to open an application in another user's context, which means that the settings and privileges imposed upon an application are those associated with the specified account. This is especially useful when running services or other background applications, where you can't always assume which user will be logged on at any time, but you want to make sure the settings and permissions are correct. Run As takes the following parameters:

```
runas [/noprofile] [/env] [/netonly] /user:username
program
```

Option	Description
program	The full path and filename of the .exe file to run.
/user:username	The user name of the form user@domain or domain\user.
/noprofile	Don't load the user's profile (in HKEY_CURRENT_USER).
/env	Uses the current environment space instead of username's.
/netonly	Specifies that specified credentials are for remote access only.

 TIP The Scheduled Tasks feature also lets you run applications under a different user account.

Scanners and Cameras
Control Panel → [Printers and Other Hardware] → Scanners and Cameras

The Scanners and Cameras window lists any digital cameras or scanners attached to the system. Configure a digital camera here to use a Windows interface to retreive pictures from the camera's memory card. Configure a scanner to choose what happens when one of the scanner's buttons are pressed (if present). Note that most scanners and cameras come with their own dedicated software, and many devices don't come with drivers that are compatible with this feature, so it's not strictly necessary to use this window at all.

Scheduled Tasks

Control Panel → [Performance and Maintenance] → Scheduled Tasks
Start → All Programs → Accessories → System Tools → Scheduled Tasks

The Scheduled Tasks feature allows you to schedule any program or WSH script to run at a specified time or repeat at some regular interval. To create a new scheduled task, open the Scheduled Tasks folder, and double-click Add Scheduled Task. Follow the prompts, or simply press Next repeatedly, until you reach the last page, at which point you'll be able to configure the task with a more convenient Properties dialog.

> **TIP** Scheduled tasks will not be performed if you've selected the Stop Using Task Scheduler option, if your computer is turned off, if Windows isn't running, or if your portable computer is running off its battery.

Shutdown

\windows\system32\shutdown.exe

Shutdown is used to perform a graceful shutdown of the computer from the command line, useful if you wish to automate the shutdown of the computer, or if you need to shut down and you don't have access to the Start menu. This tool can be used to shut down the computer with a Windows shortcut, from a WSH script or batch file, via Scheduled Tasks, from within Safe Mode with command prompt, or remotely using a Telnet client. Shutdown uses the following command-line parameters:

```
shutdown command [-m \\name] [-t n] [-c "text"] [-f]
```

Option	Description
command	Command can be one of the following:
	- i Interactive mode; displays the Shutdown dialog.
	- l Logs off (cannot be used with -m); may produce undesired effects, such as services unexpectedly stopping.
	- s Shuts down the computer.
	- r Restarts the computer.
	- a Aborts a timed system shutdown in progress.
-m \\ name	Shuts down remote computer name; does not work with - l.

Option	Description
-t *n*	Sets a timed countdown before the shutdown is performed. The default is 30 seconds; use 0 to shut down immediately.
-c "*text*"	Specifies a text message to be shown to other currently logged-on users while the countdown commences.
-f	Forces running applications to close without warning.

To perform a simple shutdown after a 30-second warning, type shutdown -s. To restart the computer without any countdown, type shutdown -r -t 0.

Solitaire

\windows\system32\sol.exe

Start → All Programs → Games → Solitaire

Solitaire is a single-player card game that follows the traditional Klondike rules. The object of the game is to organize all the cards by suit, and place them, in order (starting with the ace), in the four stacks at the top of the window. Cards are moved by placing them on the seven piles in sequential descending order, alternating color. For example, place a black 4 on a red 5, or a red Jack on a black Queen. The game is over when all the cards have been moved to the top stacks.

TIP To cheat, press Ctrl-Alt-Shift while you draw cards in a Draw-3 game to draw only a single card.

Sound Recorder

\windows\system32\sndrec32.exe

Start → All Programs → Accessories → Entertainment → Sound Recorder

Sound Recorder is used to record simple sound clips of up to one minute in length and play them back. It supports standard sound (.*wav*) files used in Control Panel → [Sounds, Speech, and Audio Devices] → Sounds and Audio Devices and hundreds of other applications. Its controls are just like those you'd find on a VCR or tape deck, including the standard rewind, fast forward, play, stop, and record.

Sounds and Audio Devices

\windows\system\mmsys.cpl

Control Panel → [Sounds, Speech, and Audio Devices] → Sounds and Audio Devices

Settings affecting the sounds Windows generates are divided into four sections: Volume (see Volume Control), Sounds (for configuring sounds for different events, such as Windows startup), Audio and Voice, for options affecting the recording of sound, and Hardware (see Device Manager). All settings in this dialog are documented in Part .

Speech Properties

Control Panel → [Sounds, Speech, and Audio Devices] → Accessibility Options

This dialog controls the text-to-speech translation (speech synthesizer) feature in Windows XP, used in conjunction with the Narrator utility. The Speech Properties dialog is used to adjust the tone and speed of the "voice" that is used. Try different voices and speeds, using Preview Voice to test them out, until you've found the best combination.

Spider Solitaire

\windows\system32\spider.exe

Spider Solitaire is a simple card game, similar to Solitaire. The object is to arrange the cards sequentially and by suit. Move cards by placing them on the eight piles in descending order, following suit. For example, place the Jack of Spades on the Queen of Spades, or the 2 of Hearts on the 3 of Hearts. When you complete an entire suit, King to Ace, it is removed from the board. The game ends when all cards have been removed. The game is played with 52 cards, but easier skill levels reduce the number of suits.

Subst

\windows\system32\subst.exe

Subst creates a new drive letter and actively links it to an existing folder on your hard disk. For example, type:

```
subst m: c:\downloaded music\oldies\metallica
```

to create a new drive letter, *m:*, and link it to the folder, *c:\ downloaded music\oldies\metallica*. When you open drive *m:* in Explorer, you'll see the contents of the linked folder, useful if you access a particular folder frequently but find Windows Shortcuts too limiting. For example, a drive created with Subst allows you to access a file in the folder, like this: *m:\astronomy.mp3*. To disconnect a Subst'd drive, type subst z: /d.

> **TIP** Drive letters created with Subst are forgotten when the computer shuts down. To have drives re-Subst'd every time you turn on your computer, write a batch file or WSH script and place it in your Startup folder.

Synchronization Manager   *\windows\system32\mobsync.exe*

Start → All Programs → Accessories → Synchronize
Internet Explorer → Tools menu → Synchronize

The Synchronization Manager synchronizes offline files and prepares remote files for offline use. The main window lists the files and folders currently set up for offline use, but you can't add new offline files here. Instead, use the following procedure:

1. Files are placed in a folder that is shared over the network.

2. A remote user right-clicks a file or folder and selects Make Available Offline.

3. The remote user then begins to edit the file, and continues to edit the file after being disconnected from the network.

4. Later on, the user reconnects to the network, and uses the Synchronization Manager to update the remote file with the one that has been edited.

5. If the Synchronization Manager finds that the file has been modified by another user since it was last accessed, a warning appears, preventing data lost by two users inadvertently editing the same file.

System Properties   *\windows\system32\sysdm.cpl*

Control Panel → [Performance and Maintenance] → System
right-click on the My Computer icon → Properties

The System Properties window contains settings that affect hardware, system performance, networking, and other Windows features. The tabs in this dialog are shown in Table 4. All the settings in this dialog are documented in Part .

Table 4. An overview of the tabs in System Properties

Tab	Description and tips
General	Displays the current Windows version, the edition, the registered user, the speed of the processor, and the amount of memory.
Computer Name	Choose how your computer is identified on your network, such as the computer's name and whether you're connected to a Windows NT domain system (referred to as a business network here).
Hardware	Contains links to the Add Hardware Wizard, Device Manager, Driver Signing Options, and the Hardware Profiles dialog.
Advanced	Go to Performance → Settings → Visual Effects tab to selectively disable several enhanced display features, such as shadows under menus and the animation of several screen elements. Go to Performance → Settings → Advanced tab to choose how memory is allocated to applications, and how Windows uses virtual memory. Go to Startup and Recovery → Settings to manage the boot manager, the mechanism responsible for booting to multiple operating systems. Error Reporting is used to disable the dialog that appears after a crash prompting you to send a "report" to Microsoft.
System Restore	See "System Restore," later in this chapter.
Automatic Updates	Windows can automatically and routinely activate the Windows Update feature to see if any updates to Windows XP exist, and optionally install them without prompting.
Remote	See "Remote Desktop," earlier in this chapter.

System Information

\windows\system32\winmsd.exe

Start → All Programs → Accessories → System tools → System Information

Microsoft System Information is a reporting tool used to view information about hardware, system resources used by that hardware, software drivers, and Internet Explorer settings. Information is arranged in a familiar Explorer-like tree. Expand or collapse branches with the plus [+] and minus [–] signs, and click any category to view the corresponding information in the righthand pane.

System Restore

\windows\system32\restore\rstrui.exe

Start → All Programs → Accessories → System Tools → System Restore
System Information → Tools menu → System Restore

System Restore is a feature that runs invisibly in the background, continuously backing up important system files and registry settings. The idea is that at some point, you may wish to roll back your computer's configuration to a time before things started going wrong. By default, System Restore is turned on, using up to 12% of your computer's hard disk space.

To configure System Restore, click "System Restore Settings" in the main System Restore window, or go to Control Panel → [Performance and Maintenance] → System → System Restore tab.

WARNING

System Restore indiscriminately replaces files installed in your computer with potentially earlier versions, resets registry preferences, and in some cases, uninstalls software. While the intention is to solve some problems, it can inadvertently cause others. If you suspect that a particular application is causing a problem, your best bet is to uninstall that single application rather than attempting a System Restore. Use System Restore as a last resort only.

Task Manager *\windows\system32\taskmgr.exe*

Ctrl-Alt-Del → Task Manager
right-click on empty portion of Taskbar → Task Manager
keyboard shortcut: Ctrl-Shift-Esc

Task Manager displays a list of currently running programs, background processes, and some performance statistics. The Applications tab shows all foreground applications their statuses select any item and click End Task to close any hung applications. The Processes tab is similar, but also includes background applications and services, providing a more complete view of what your computer is doing at any instant. The Performance tab shows several graphs, all updated in real time, used to monitor the performance of the system. Finally, the Networking tab shows real-time graphs depicting the performance of your network connections.

Taskbar and Start Menu Properties

Control Panel → [Appearance and Themes] → Taskbar and Start Menu
right-click on an empty portion of the Taskbar → Properties
right-click on the Start button → Properties
Start → Settings → Taskbar and Start Menu (Classic Start Menu only)

Use this dialog to change the appearance and behavior of the Taskbar, notification area (commonly known as the tray), and Start Menu. All the settings here are listed in Part .

Probably the most important setting here is the choice between the new XP-style, two-column Start Menu and the simpler, "Classic" single-column Start menu found in earlier versions of Windows. Click Customize to selectively show or hide certain items in the Start Menu, appropriate to the style you've chosen.

Taskkill *\windows\system32\taskkill.exe*

Taskkill, included with Windows XP Professional only, is used to end one or more running processes from the command line. Task Manager, described previously, provides a more convenient interface for this function, but Taskkill can be used remotely. Taskkill takes the following command-line parameters:

```
taskkill [/s system [/u [domain\]username
    [/p [password]]]] [/pid process_id | /im image]
    [/f] [/t]
```

Option	Description
/s system	Specifies the remote system to which to connect.
/u [domain\] username	Specifies the user context under which to execute.
/p [password]	Specifies the password for the specified user.
/f	Forcefully terminates the process.
/pid process_id	Specifies the process ID of the process to be terminated. To obtain the process IDs, use Tasklist (later in this chapter).
/im image	Specifies the image name of the process to be terminated; specify * to terminate all image names.
/t	Terminates the specified process and process tree, which includes any child processes that were started by it.

Tasklist

\windows\system32\tasklist.exe

Tasklist is used to list running processes from the command line. Tasklist works together with Taskkill, discussed earlier in this chapter, to provide command-line equivalents to the functionality provided by the Processes tab in Task Manager. Tasklist takes the following command-line parameters:

```
tasklist [/s system [/u username [/p [password]]]]
    [/m [module] | /svc | /v] [/fi filter]
    [/fo format] [/nh]
```

The /s, /u, and /p options are identical to those documented under Taskkill, earlier in this chapter.

Option	Description
/m [module]	Lists all tasks that have DLL modules loaded that match the pattern, module. If module is omitted, all modules are shown.
/svc	Displays the services in each process.
/v	Verbose mode; display all available information.
/fi filter	Filter the task list with the specified criteria.

Option	Description
/fo *format*	Specifies the format of the display: type /fo table (the default) for a formatted table, /fo list, for a plaint text list, or /fo csv for a comma-separated report, suitable for importing into a spreadsheet or database.
/nh	Turns off the column headers.

Telnet

\windows\system32\telnet.exe

Telnet is used to connect to a remote computer. A Telnet session works very much like a command prompt window, except that commands entered are executed on the remote machine. What you do in Telnet depends on the platform of the remote machine; for example, if connecting to a Unix host, you'll get a standard terminal window. If you connect to a Windows host, you'll get a DOS command-prompt window.

If you launch Telnet without any options, you'll get a prompt, at which you can type commands such as open *server_name* to initiate a connection or quit to end the session. To launch Telnet and connect automatically, type telnet *server_name* [port] or telnet: //*server_name*:port.

Tracert

\windows\system32\tracert.exe

This tool is used to trace the route of communcation across the Internet to another computer, reporting the name of each intermediate machine it encounters along the way. For example, type tracert microsoft.com to show how your signal hops from computer to computer in its jorney to Microsoft's web site. Tracert accepts the following options:

    tracert [-d] [-h *max_hops*] [-j *list*] [-w *timeout*] target

Option	Description
target	The name or IP address of the computer to contact.
-d	If you specify an IP address, Tracert will attempt to resolve the host name (using NSLookup). Include the -d option to skip this step.
-h *max_hops*	Specifies the maximum number of "hops" (servers along the route) to display before giving up; the default is 30 hops.

Option	Description
-j *list*	Loosely imposes a route to follow, where *list* is a list of hosts.
-w *timeout*	Sets the amount of time to wait (in milliseconds) for each reply.

User Accounts

\windows\system32\nusrmgr.cpl

Control Panel → User Accounts

The User Accounts window lets you add or remove user accounts, change the privileges of existing users, and choose how users log on and off. Click Change an account to change your password or choose a new icon to appear in the Start Menu and Welcome screen. Use Create a new account to add an account for a new user, either to be used by someone sitting down in front of your machine, or someone connecting remotely with a Remote Desktop or accessing your files and printers with My Network Places. Finally, click Change the way users log on or off to choose between the new Welcome screen and the more traditional logon screen. All the settings in this dialog are also covered in Part .

Utility Manager

\windows\system32\utilman.exe

Start → All Programs → Accessories → Accessibility → Utility Manager
keyboard shortcut: ⊞ + U

The Utility Manager application allows you to control the Magnifier, Narrator, and On-Screen Keyboard—all of which are discussed earlier this chapter—from one central location. Use the Utility Manager to start or stop the accessibility tools, or configure Windows to start any or all of them automatically when you log in, when you lock your Desktop, or when the Utility Manager starts.

Volume Control

\windows\system32\sndvol32.exe

Start → All Programs → Accessories → Entertainment → Volume Control
Tray → Double-click yellow speaker icon (if it's there)

Volume Control displays volume and balance adjustments for all the different sound devices, such as the audio CD volume, microphone volume, and line-in volume. To choose the controls that are shown, or to hide those you never use, go to Options → Properties, and select any of the following (note that different sounds drivers may omit some of these, or even add additional entries).

> **TIP** To turn on or off the volume control on the taskbar, go to Control Panel → [Sounds, Speech, and Audio Devices] → Sounds and Audio Devices → Volume tab and turn on the "Place volume icon in the taskbar" option.

Windows Explorer
\windows\explorer.exe

Start → All Programs → Accessories → Windows Explorer
Double-click My Computer or any folder icon on the Desktop or in any folder window

Windows Explorer is the default Windows interface, responsible for the Start Menu, the Desktop, the Taskbar, the Search tool, the Windows Explorer window, and all folder windows. See Part for basic navigation and file management principles, and Part for the settings that affect Explorer. Explorer accepts the following command-line options (note the mandatory commas):

```
explorer.exe [/n] [/e] [,/root,object]
    [[/select],subobject]
```

Option	Description
/n	Forces Explorer to open a new window.
/e	Display the Folders Explorer Bar (folder tree).
[/select], subobject	Include subobject to specify the file or folder to be initially highlighted or expanded when the folder is opened.
,/root,object	Specifies a different root for the folder tree; object can be the full path to a folder or a class ID to a system object.

Examples

```
explorer /n, /e, /select, c:\
explorer /e,/root,c:\Documents and Settings\username
```

TIP	Explorer allows you to burn CDs, provided that you have a CD writer. Start by right-clicking on the drive icon for your CD recorder, selecting Properties, choosing the Recording tab, and making sure the "Enable CD recording on this drive" option is turned on. Then, drag-drop files and folders onto the drive as though it were just another hard disk. When you're done, right-click the drive icon and select Write these files to CD.

Windows IP Configuration

\windows\system32\ipconfig.exe

The Windows IP Configuration tool, used without any options, displays your computer's current IP address, subnet mask, and default gateway. This information can also be viewed by double-clicking a connection in the Network Connections window.

Windows IP Configuration takes the following parameters:

```
ipconfig [/command] [adapter]
```

Command	Description
/all	Displays all available configuration information.
/release [adapter]	Releases the IP address(es) for the specified connection, disconnecting it from all network communication. See /renew.
/renew [adapter]	Reestablishes communication for the connection.
/flushdns	Purges the DNS cache. See NSLookup, earlier in this chapter. See see /displaydns to show the DNS cache.
/registerdns	Refreshes all DHCP leases and reregisters DNS names
/displaydns	Displays the contents of the DNS Resolver Cache (see /flushdns).
/showclassid adapter	Displays all the DHCP class IDs allowed for adapter.
/setclassid adapter [classid]	Modifies the DHCP class ID for adapter.

Windows Media Player   *\program files\windows media player\wmplayer.exe;*
\windows\system32\mplay32.exe

Start → All Programs → Accessories → Entertainment → Windows Media Player

Windows Media Player is the default application used to open and play most of the types of video and audio media, such as *.mpg* movies, *.mp3* songs, audio CD tracks, and *.asf* streaming media. Just double-click an associated media file to open Media Player and then use the VCR-like controls to play, stop, rewind, etc. Features of note include the Radio Tuner, which allows you to listen to radio webcasts, the built-in CD burner support, which allows you to make audio CDs from playlists, and integrated DVD player that plays full DVD movies, provided that you have a DVD-ROM drive.

Windows Messenger   *\program files\messenger\msmsgs.exe*

Start → All Programs → Windows Messenger

Windows Messenger allows users to send each other quick text messages over the Internet by maintaining an open connection to a central directory server. That server links a user's "screen name" with their IP address (which can change every time that user connects to the Internet), necessary for establishing direct communication between two computers. To use Windows Messenger or MSN Explorer, you'll be required to set up a Microsoft .NET Passport account.

> **TIP**   Windows Messenger, by default, is started every time Windows is started, regardless of whether you use it or even have an account. To disable Windows Messenger, open the Registry Editor (described in Part) and remove the corresponding entry from HKEY_LOCAL_MACHINE\SOFTWARE\Microsoft\ Windows\CurrentVersion\Run.

Windows Movie Maker   *\program files\movie maker\moviemk.exe*

Start → All Programs → Accessories → Windows Movie Maker

The Windows Movie Maker allows you to edit and convert video clips, and if you have video capture hardware or a digital video camera, you can even create your own video clips. Video editors don't work like most other applications. Instead of opening files, making changes to them, and then saving them, a typical video editing session works something like this:

1. Start a new project by going to File → New → Project, and then add one or more existing video files to the project by going to File → Import. Supported formats include *.asf*, *.avi*, *.wmv*, *.mpg* movies, *.wav* and *.snd* audio files, and *.bmp*, *.jpg*, and *.gif* still image files. All imported videos are then shown in the Collections pane; click a video filename to display "clips," arbitrary divisions in the file inserted by Movie Maker.

2. The actual video project consists of clips inserted into the timeline, the storyboard-style pane at the bottom of the window. To add a clip to the timeline, drag it from the Collections pane and drop it at the desired location. Go to Clip → Split (or press Ctrl-Shift-S) to break apart the current video clip into two discrete clips. Once you've split a clip, you can delete or rearrange the segments as desired.

3. Click the Play button to preview the video project, and then go to File → Save Movie to create a new video file based on your work in the timeline.

Windows Picture and Fax Viewer

The Windows Picture and Fax Viewer isn't a standalone application in the traditional sense, but rather a simple viewer window. For a better image viewer, try ACDSee-32 (*http://www.acdsee.com*) or Paint Shop Pro (*http://www.jasc.com*). You could even assocate image files with your web browser.

| TIP | When Windows XP is first installed, the Windows Picture and Fax Viewer is the default viewer for these image formats: *.emf*, *.gif*, *.jpeg*, *.bmp*, *.png*, *.tif*, and *.wmf*. Unfortunately, making another program the default image viewer will not disable the Windows Picture and Fax Viewer. To remedy this, open the Registry Editor, go to `HKEY_CLASSES_ROOT\SystemFileAssociations\image\ShellEx\ContextMenuHandlers`, and delete the `ShellImagePreview` key entirely. |

Windows Update

\windows\system32\wupdmgr.exe

Start → Windows Update
Internet Explorer → Tools menu → Windows Update

This feature uses Internet Explorer to selectively download
updates to Windows XP from Microsoft's web site, and install
them automatically. Activate Windows Update (or navigate to
http://www.windowsupdate.com) and then click Scan for updates
to list the available updates that havn't yet been installed. There
are three categories of updates: "Critical Updates," typically new
versions of shared files that fix problems and patch security holes,
"Windows XP," which contains new versions of some of the
components discussed in this chapter, and "Driver Updates,"
which lists any newer versions of Microsoft drivers you may have
installed on your system.

> **TIP** To configure the automatic update feature, go to
> Control Panel → [Performance and Maintenance] →
> System → Automatic Updates tab.

WordPad

\program files\windows nt\wordpad.exe

Start → All Programs → Accessories → WordPad

Although WordPad lacks many of the features that come with
full-blown word processors such as Wordperfect or Microsoft
Word, it has enough features to create and edit rich-text documents. WordPad is the default editor for *.rtf*, *.doc*, and *.wri* files
(unless Microsoft Word is installed). WordPad can also be used to
edit plain text files (*.txt*), although Notepad (discussed earlier this
chapter) is the default and is more appropriate for this task.

PART IV

Setting Index

After a quick assessment of Windows XP, it should become apparent that there are literally hundreds of settings, features, and displays of information, and finding these items in the interface can sometimes be a challenge.

This section provides a comprehensive listing of more than 700 entries, all of which are accessible with components listed in Part III, but sorted alphabetically by their function rather than by their location in the operating system interface. For example, to find out how to turn off the Power Management icon in the Taskbar Notification Area, look under "Taskbar Notification Area, Power Icon." A few settings have been duplicated with different labels to make them easier to find, so you'll also find this setting under "Advanced Power Management, icon in Notification Area (tray)."

Alphabetical List of Windows XP Settings

In this section, we've used some shorthand to keep the table as concise as possible. Entries that start with an ellipsis (...) fall under the same category as the preceding non-ellipsis entry.

Setting	Location
Accessibility, additional settings for web pages	Control Panel → Internet Options → General tab → Accessibility
...enable/disable warnings & notifications	Control Panel → Accessibility Options → General tab

Setting	Location
…move Magnifier with focus change in web pages	Control Panel → Internet Options → Advanced tab → Accessibility → Move system caret with focus/ selection changes
Address bar, Go button	See "Go button"
…history settings	Control Panel → Internet Options → General tab → History section
…search settings	Control Panel → Internet Options → Advanced tab → Search from the Address bar
…show in Explorer	Explorer → View → Toolbars → Address Bar
…show on taskbar	Right-click on empty area of taskbar → Toolbars → Address
…show the full path of current folder	Control Panel → Folder Options → View tab → Display the full path in the address bar
Address Book, make the default contact list	Control Panel → Internet Options → Programs tab → Contact list
…profile assistant (enable/ disable)	Control Panel → Internet Options → Advanced tab → Security → Enable Profile Assistant
…set default profile for AutoComplete	Control Panel → Internet Options → Content tab → My Profile
Administrative Tools, show in Start Menu (Classic Start Menu only)	Control Panel → Taskbar and Start Menu → Start Menu tab → Customize → "Advanced Start menu options" section → Display Administrative Tools
…show in Start Menu (XP Start Menu only)	Control Panel → Taskbar and Start Menu → Start Menu tab → Customize → Advanced tab → "Start menu items" section → System Administrative Tools
Advanced Power Management, additional settings	Your computer's BIOS setup
…effect on Offline files	Explorer → Tools → Synchronize → Setup → On Idle tab → Advanced → Prevent synchronization when my computer is running on battery power
…effect on Scheduled Tasks	Control Panel → Scheduled Tasks → right-click task → Properties → Settings tab → Power Management section
…enable/disable	Control Panel → Power Options → APM tab → Enable Advanced Power Management support

Setting	Location
...icon in notification area (tray)	Control Panel → Power Options → Advanced tab → Always show icon on the taskbar
Alt Key, make it "sticky"	Control Panel → Accessibility Options → Keyboard tab → Use StickyKeys
Animation, enable/disable selectively	Control Panel → System → Advanced tab → Performance section → Settings → Visual Effects tab → Custom TweakUI → General
...fading between web pages	Control Panel → Internet Options → Advanced tab → Browsing → Enable page transitions
...show animated GIFs in web pages	Control Panel → Internet Options → Advanced tab → Multimedia → Play animations in web pages
...smooth scrolling of lists	TweakUI → Explorer → Enable smooth scrolling
...smooth scrolling of web pages	Control Panel → Internet Options → Advanced tab → Browsing → Use smooth scrolling
Applications, ending	Task Manager (*taskmgr.exe*) → Applications tab
...ending background processes	Task Manager (*taskmgr.exe*) → Processes tab
...list loaded DLLs	System Information (*winmsd.exe*) → Software Environment → Loaded Modules
AutoComplete, edit data	Control Panel → Internet Options → Content tab → My Profile
...enable/disable	Control Panel → Internet Options → Advanced tab → Browsing → Use inline AutoComplete
...Profile Assistant (enable/disable)	Control Panel → Internet Options → Advanced tab → Security → Enable Profile Assistant
...settings	Control Panel → Internet Options → Content tab → AutoComplete
Autodial	See "Dialing"
Autoexec.bat, parse at logon	TweakUI → Logon
Automatic Windows Update settings	Control Panel → System → Automatic Updates tab
Autoplay	Explorer → right-click CD drive icon → Properties → AutoPlay tab TweakUI → My Computer → AutoPlay

Setting	Location
Background, create and modify	Paint (*mspaint.exe*) → save as .bmp in Windows folder
…select and configure	Control Panel → Display → Desktop tab
Balloon tips (big Tooltips that pop up from taskbar notification area)	TweakUI → Taskbar → Enable balloon tips
Browser, set default	Control Panel → Internet Options → Programs tab → Internet Explorer should check to see whether it is the default browser
Button color	Control Panel → Display → Appearance tab → Advanced → Item list → choose "3d Objects"
Calendar, default application	Control Panel → Internet Options → Programs tab → Calendar
Calling	See "Dialing"
Cascading Style Sheets	See "Style Sheets"
CD, autoplay	See "Autoplay"
CD Burning, folder location	TweakUI → My Computer → Special Folders
Certificates, check for revocation in Internet Explorer	Control Panel → Internet Options → Advanced tab → Security
…Internet Explorer settings for secure sites	Control Panel → Internet Options → Content tab → Certificates section
…warn about invalid certificates in Internet Explorer	Control Panel → Internet Options → Advanced tab → Security → Warn about invalid site certificates
Clock, show on the taskbar	Control Panel → Taskbar and Start Menu → Taskbar tab → Show the clock
Code page conversion table	Control Panel → Regional and Language Options → Advanced tab → Code page conversion tables
Color profiles, associate with device	Right-click on *.icm* file → Properties → Associate Device tab
…management	Control Panel → Display → Settings tab → Advanced → Color Management tab
Colors, change for all display elements	Control Panel → Display → Appearance tab → Advanced

Setting	Location
...encrypted and compressed files	TweakUI → Explorer → Colors
...in web pages	Control Panel → Internet Options → General tab → Colors
...increase or decrease number of supported colors (color depth)	Control Panel → Display → Settings tab → Color Quality
...show high contrast screen colors	Control Panel → Accessibility Options → Display tab → Use High Contrast
Combo boxes, enable/ disable animation	Control Panel → System → Advanced tab → Performance section → Settings → Visual Effects tab → Custom
Command keys, customize	TweakUI → Explorer → Command Keys
Command prompt, filename completion	TweakUI → Command Prompt
...settings	Command Prompt window → Control Menu
Compressed NTFS files, choose color	TweakUI → Explorer → Colors
...differentiate with a different color	Control Panel → Folder Options → View tab → Show encrypted or compressed NTFS files in color
Contact list, default	Control Panel → Internet Options → Programs tab → Contact list
Control Panel, security policies	Group Policy (*gpedit.msc*) → User Configuration → Administrative Templates → Control Panel
...categories (show/hide)	Control Panel → Tools → Options → General tab → Show common tasks in folders → OK → Switch to Classic View or Switch to Category View
...icons (show/hide)	TweakUI → Control Panel
...show as menu in Start Menu (Classic Start Menu only)	Control Panel → Taskbar and Start Menu → Start Menu tab → Customize → "Advanced Start menu options" section → Expand Control Panel
...show as menu in Start Menu (XP Start Menu only)	Control Panel → Taskbar and Start Menu → Start Menu tab → Customize → Advanced tab → "Start menu items" section → Control Panel
...show in My Computer	Control Panel → Folder Options → View tab → Show Control Panel in My Computer TweakUI → My Computer

Setting	Location
Cookies, change settings (block, allow, prompt)	Control Panel → Internet Options → Privacy tab → Advanced → Override automatic cookie handling
...change settings for specific web sites (block, allow, prompt)	Control Panel → Internet Options → Privacy tab → Edit
...delete all	Control Panel → Internet Options → General tab → Temporary Internet Files section → Delete Cookies
Country, choose for dialing preferences	Control Panel → Phone and Modem Options → Dialing Rules tab → select location → Edit → Country/region
...choose for localized information	Control Panel → Regional and Language Options → Regional Options tab → Location section
Crashes, send reports to Microsoft	Control Panel → System → Advanced tab → Error Reporting
Critical Update Notification	Control Panel → System → Automatic Updates tab
Ctrl Key, make it "sticky"	Control Panel → Accessibility Options → Keyboard tab → Use StickyKeys
Ctrl-Alt-Del window, settings	Group Policy (*gpedit.msc*) → User Configuration → Administrative Templates → System → Ctrl+Alt+Del Options
Currency, customize display	Control Panel → Regional and Language Options → Regional Options tab → Customize → Currency tab
Date, customize display	Control Panel → Regional and Language Options → Regional Options tab → Customize → Date tab
...set	Control Panel → Date and Time → Date & Time tab
Daylight Savings, enable/disable	Control Panel → Date and Time → Time Zone tab
Desktop, Cleanup Wizard runs every 60 days	Control Panel → Display → Desktop tab → Customize Desktop → General tab → Run Desktop Cleanup every 60 days
...color	Control Panel → Display → Desktop tab → Color Control Panel → Display → Appearance tab → Advanced → Item list → choose "Desktop"
...folder, change location	TweakUI → My Computer → Special Folders
...icons	See "Icons"
...refresh	Click on an empty portion of the Desktop → press F5

Setting	Location
...restrict installation of items	Control Panel → Internet Options → Security tab → Custom Level
...security policies	Group Policy (*gpedit.msc*) → User Configuration → Administrative Templates → Desktop
...show contents without minimizing applications	Right-click on taskbar → Toolbars → Show Desktop Right-click on taskbar → Toolbars → Show Open Windows (to restore) Explorer → open Desktop folder
...version (show/hide)	TweakUI → General → Show Windows version on Desktop
...web content (enable/disable)	TweakUI → Explorer → Allow Web content to be added to the Desktop
...web content, lock	TweakUI → Explorer → Lock Web content
...web pages, add/remove/hide	Control Panel → Display → Desktop tab → Customize Desktop → Web tab
...web pages, allow moving and resizing	Control Panel → Display → Desktop tab → Customize Desktop → Web tab → Lock Desktop items
...web pages, automatic download of linked pages	Control Panel → Display → Desktop tab → Customize Desktop → Web tab → select item → Properties → Download tab
...web pages, automatic updates	Control Panel → Display → Desktop tab → Customize Desktop → Web tab → select item → Properties → Schedule tab
...web pages, automatic updates (enable/disable)	Control Panel → Internet Options → Advanced tab → Browsing → Enable offline items to be synchronized on a schedule
Devices	See "Hardware"
Dialing, area code settings	Control Panel → Phone and Modem Options → Dialing Rules tab → select location → Edit
...call waiting	Control Panel → Phone and Modem Options → Dialing Rules tab → select location → Edit → General tab → To disable call waiting...
...calling card	Control Panel → Phone and Modem Options → Dialing Rules tab → select location → Edit → Calling Card tab
...connect to the Internet when needed	Control Panel → Internet Options → Connection tab → Dial whenever/Always dial

Setting	Location
…connect to the Internet when needed, depending on location	Control Panel → Network Connections → Advanced → Dial-Up Preferences
…default Internet connection	Control Panel → Internet Options → Connection tab → select connection → Set Default
…disconnect Internet connection when no longer needed	Control Panel → Internet Options → Connection tab → select connection → Settings
…operator-assisted	Control Panel → Network Connections → Advanced → Operator-Assisted Dialing
Digital Camera, add as drive in Explorer (still camera only)	Control Panel → Scanners and Cameras → Add Device
Disconnect from Internet automatically	Control Panel → Internet Options → Connection tab → select connection → Settings
Display, force restart after changing resolution or color depth	Control Panel → Display → Settings tab → Advanced → General tab → Compatibility section
…list all possible combinations of resolution and color depth	Control Panel → Display → Settings tab → Advanced → Adapter tab → List All Modes
…refresh rate	Control Panel → Display → Settings tab → Advanced → Monitor tab → Screen refresh rate
…resolution	Control Panel → Display → Settings tab → Screen resolution
…show amount of memory installed on display adapter	Control Panel → Display → Settings tab → Advanced → Adapter tab → Adapter Information section
…size	Control Panel → Display → Settings tab → Screen resolution
…style	Control Panel → Display → Appearance tab → Windows and buttons list
…style, apply to controls in web pages	Control Panel → Internet Options → Advanced tab → Browsing → Enable visual styles on buttons and controls in web pages
…troubleshooting	Control Panel → Display → Settings tab → Advanced → Troubleshoot tab
…turn off to save power	Control Panel → Power Options → Power Schemes tab → Turn off hard disks

Setting	Location
Document templates, manage	TweakUI → Templates
...relocate folder	TweakUI → My Computer → Special Folders
Documents, history, clear on exit	TweakUI → Explorer → Clear document history on exit
...history, maintain	TweakUI → Explorer → Maintain document history
...show on Start Menu (Classic Start Menu only)	TweakUI → Explorer → Show My Documents on classic Start Menu
...show on Start Menu (XP Start Menu only)	TweakUI → Explorer → Allow Recent Documents on Start Menu
Double-click required to open icons	Control Panel → Folder Options → General tab → Double-click to open an item
Download Complete message, enable/disable	Control Panel → Internet Options → Advanced tab → Browsing → Notify when downloads complete
Drives, show/hide in My Computer	TweakUI → My Computer → Drives
...warn when low on free space	TweakUI → Taskbar → Warn when low on disk space
DVD drive, autoplay enable/disable	Explorer → right-click DVD drive icon → Properties → AutoPlay tab
Effects, display settings	Control Panel → Display → Appearance tab → Effects
Email icon, show in Start Menu (XP Start Menu only)	Control Panel → Taskbar and Start Menu → Start Menu tab → Customize → General tab → E-mail
Email program, default	Control Panel → Internet Options → Programs tab → E-mail
Encrypted NTFS files, customize color	TweakUI → Explorer → Colors
...differentiate with a different color	Control Panel → Folder Options → View tab → Show encrypted or compressed NTFS files in color
...use with Offline files	Control Panel → Folder Options → Offline Files tab → Encrypt offline files to secure data
Environment variables	Control Panel → System → Advanced tab → Environment variables
Error messages, font	Control Panel → Display → Appearance tab → Advanced → Item list → choose "Message Box"

Setting	Location
...sound	Control Panel → Sounds and Audio Devices → Sounds tab
...text color	Control Panel → Display → Appearance tab → Advanced → Item list → choose "Window"
Error Reporting, advanced settings	Group Policy (*gpedit.msc*) → Computer Configuration → Administrative Templates → System → Error Reporting
...enable/disable	Control Panel → System → Advanced tab → Error Reporting
Explorer	See "Windows Explorer"
Extensions, show/hide filename extensions	Control Panel → Folder Options → View tab → Hide extensions for known file types
Favorites, hide infrequently used items	Control Panel → Internet Options → Advanced tab → Browsing → Enable Personalized Favorites Menu
...links (show/hide)	TweakUI → Explorer → Show Links on Favorites menu
...navigation key	TweakUI → Explorer → Command Keys
...relocate folder	TweakUI → My Computer → Special Folders
...show in Start Menu (Classic Start Menu only)	Control Panel → Taskbar and Start Menu → Start Menu tab → Customize → "Advanced Start menu options" section → Display Favorites
...show in Start Menu (XP Start Menu only)	Control Panel → Taskbar and Start Menu → Start Menu tab → Customize → Advanced tab → "Start menu items" section → Favorites menu
Fax service, install support	Control Panel → Printers and Faxes → File → Set Up Faxing
File dialogs, options	TweakUI → Common Dialogs
Files, differentiate encrypted or compressed NTFS files with a different color	Control Panel → Folder Options → View tab → Show encrypted or compressed NTFS files in color
...display size in folder tips	Control Panel → Folder Options → View tab → Display file size information in folder tips
...double-click sensitivity	TweakUI → Mouse
...downloads (enable/disable)	Control Panel → Internet Options → Security tab → Custom Level
...drag-drop (enable/disable)	Control Panel → Internet Options → Security tab → Custom Level

Setting	Location
…drag-drop sensitivity	TweakUI → Mouse
…extensions (show/hide)	Control Panel → Folder Options → View tab → Hide extensions for known file types
…filename completion in command prompt	TweakUI → Command Prompt
…hidden files (show/hide)	Control Panel → Folder Options → View tab → Hidden files and folders
…Indexing Service	See "Indexing Service"
…system files (show/hide)	Control Panel → Folder Options → View tab → Hide protected operating system files
Firewall	See "Internet Connection Firewall"
Focus, prevent applications from stealing	TweakUI → General → Focus
Folders, cache settings for offline access	Explorer → right-click folder icon → Sharing → Caching
…close automatically when Favorites or History folder is shown	Control Panel → Internet Options → Advanced tab → Browsing → Close unused folders in History and Favorites
…columns in details view	Folder window → View → Details → View → Choose Details
…display file size in folder tips	Control Panel → Folder Options → View tab → Display file size information in folder tips
…group similar items	Folder window → View Arrange Icons by → Show in Groups
…history settings	Control Panel → Internet Options → General tab → History section
…Indexing Service	See "Indexing Service"
…open each folder in its own window	Control Panel → Folder Options → General tab → Open each folder in its own window
…open in separate process	Control Panel → Folder Options → View tab → Launch folder windows in separate process
…refresh view	Folder window → View → Refresh or press F5
…remember individual settings	Control Panel → Folder Options → View tab → Remember each folder's view settings

Setting	Location
...reopen all folder windows that were left open when system was last shut down	Control Panel → Folder Options → View tab → Restore previous folder windows at logon
...reset default appearance to Windows default	Control Panel → Folder Options → View tab → Reset All Folders
...reuse folder windows	Control Panel → Folder Options → General tab → Open each folder in the same window
...reuse folder windows when launching Internet shortcuts	Control Panel → Internet Options → Advanced tab → Browsing → Reuse windows for launching shortcuts
...set default appearance	Open any folder and configure it as you wish → Tools → Folder Options → View tab → Apply to All Folders
...share on network	Explorer → right-click folder icon → Sharing → Share this folder
...show/hide hidden folders	Control Panel → Folder Options → View tab → Hidden files and folders
...show background images	Control Panel → System → Advanced tab → Performance section → Settings → Visual Effects tab → Custom
...show common tasks	Control Panel → System → Advanced tab → Performance section → Settings → Visual Effects tab → Custom
...show contents of system folders	Control Panel → Folder Options → View tab → Display the contents of system folders
...show Digital Camera memory as a folder (still camera only)	Control Panel → Scanners and Cameras → Add Device
...show FTP site as folder in Internet Explorer	Control Panel → Internet Options → Advanced tab → Browsing → Enable folder view for FTP sites
...show lines in Explorer tree view	Control Panel → Folder Options → View tab → Display simple folder view in Explorer's Folders list
...show the full path in the address bar	Control Panel → Folder Options → View tab → Display the full path in the address bar
...show the full path in the title bar	Control Panel → Folder Options → View tab → Display the full path in the title bar

Setting	Location
Fonts, change DPI of all screen fonts	Control Panel → Display → Settings tab → Advanced → General tab → DPI setting list → select "Custom setting"
...determine link between font filename and font screen name	Control Panel → Fonts → View → Details
...downloads (enable/ disable)	Control Panel → Internet Options → Security tab → Custom Level
...eliminate duplicates	Control Panel → Fonts → View → List Fonts by Similarity
...in web pages	Control Panel → Internet Options → General tab → Fonts
...in windows, menus, and icons	Control Panel → Display → Appearance tab → Advanced
...install	Control Panel → Fonts → File → Install New Font
...repair folder	TweakUI → Repair
...size in applications	Control Panel → Display → Appearance tab → Font size
...smooth edges (enable/ disable)	Control Panel → System → Advanced tab → Performance section → Settings → Visual Effects tab → Custom
...smooth edges (settings)	Control Panel → Display → Appearance tab → Effects → Use the following method to smooth edges of screen fonts
...uninstall	Control Panel → Fonts → delete a font file to uninstall it
...view & compare	Control Panel → Fonts → double-click any font
FTP, server restrictions	Control Panel → Network Connections → right-click connection → Properties → Advanced tab → Settings → Services tab
...show as folder in Internet Explorer	Control Panel → Internet Options → Advanced tab → Browsing → Enable folder view for FTP sites
...use passive mode	Control Panel → Internet Options → Advanced tab → Browsing → Use Passive FTP

Setting	Location
Go button, show in address bar	Control Panel → Internet Options → Advanced tab → Browsing → Show Go button in Address Bar Right-click on empty portion of address bar → Go Button
Hang up Internet connection automatically	Control Panel → Internet Options → Connection tab → select connection → Settings
Hard Disk, cache settings for offline access	Explorer → right-click drive icon → Sharing → Caching
...check for errors	Explorer → right-click drive icon → Properties → Tools tab → Check Now
...clean up	Explorer → right-click drive icon → Properties → General tab → Disk Cleanup
...compress drive	Explorer → right-click drive icon → Properties → Compress drive to save disk space
...convert to dynamic disk	Disk Management (*diskmgmt.msc*) → View → Top → Disk List → right-click on drive in top pane → Convert to Dynamic Disk
...defragment	Explorer → right-click drive icon → Properties → Tools tab → Defragment Now
...enable/disable write caching	Device Manager → right-click drive → Properties → Policies tab → Enable write caching on the disk
...Indexing Service	See "Indexing Service"
...list volumes	Device Manager → right-click drive → Properties → Volumes tab → Populate
...quota management	Explorer → right-click folder icon → Properties → Quota tab
...quota security policies	Group Policy (*gpedit.msc*) → Computer Configuration → Administrative Templates → System → Disk Quotas
...share on network	Explorer → right-click drive icon → Sharing → Share this folder
...turn off to save power	Control Panel → Power Options → Power Schemes tab → Turn off monitor
Hardware, change the driver for a device	Device Manager → right-click on device → Properties → Driver tab → Update Driver
...driver information for a device	Device Manager → right-click on device → Properties → Driver tab → Driver Details

Setting	Location
...driver signing options	Control Panel → System → Hardware tab → Driver Signing
...enable/disable	Device Manager → right-click on device → Properties → General tab → Device usage
...install	Control Panel → Add Hardware
...IRQ Steering settings	Device Manager → Computer → right-click sole entry → Properties → IRQ Steering tab
...list devices	System Information (*winmsd.exe*) → Components
...list drivers	System Information (*winmsd.exe*) → Software Environment
...list resources used	System Information (*winmsd.exe*) → Hardware Resources
...places to look for drivers	Group Policy (*gpedit.msc*) → User Configuration → Administrative Templates → System
...profile settings	Control Panel → System → Hardware tab → Hardware Profiles
...resources in use by a device	Device Manager → right-click on device → Properties → Resources tab
...security policies	Group Policy (*gpedit.msc*) → Computer Configuration → Windows Settings → Security Settings → Local Policies → Security Options
...show all installed devices	Device Manager
...uninstall	Device Manager → right-click on device → Uninstall
...Universal Plug and Play support	Control Panel → Network Connections → Advanced → Optional Networking Components → Networking Services
Help, pop-up help windows	See "Tooltips"
...show in Start Menu (XP Start Menu only)	Control Panel → Taskbar and Start Menu → Start Menu tab → Customize → Advanced tab → "Start menu items" section → Help and Support TweakUI → Explorer → Allow Help on Start Menu
Hibernation, enable/disable	Control Panel → Power Options → Hibernate tab → Enable hibernation
Hidden files and folders, show/hide	Control Panel → Folder Options → View tab → Hidden files and folders
Hourglass, change icon	Control Panel → Mouse → Pointers tab

Setting	Location
HTML editor, default	Control Panel → Internet Options → Programs tab → HTML Editor
Icons, Desktop icons (show/hide)	Control Panel → Display → Desktop tab → Customize Desktop TweakUI → Desktop
…highlight color & font	Control Panel → Display → Appearance tab → Advanced → Item list → choose "Selected Items"
…repair	TweakUI → Repair
…show shadows under icon captions	Control Panel → System → Advanced tab → Performance section → Settings → Visual Effects tab → Custom
…show translucent selection rectangle when highlighting multiple icons	Control Panel → System → Advanced tab → Performance section → Settings → Visual Effects tab → Custom
…single-click or double-click	Control Panel → Folder Options → General tab → Click items as follows
…size on Desktop and in folders	Control Panel → Display → Appearance tab → Effects → Use large icons Control Panel → Display → Appearance tab → Advanced → Item list → choose "Icon"
…spacing on Desktop and in folders	Control Panel → Display → Appearance tab → Advanced → Item list → choose "Icon Spacing (Horizontal)" or "Icon Spacing (Vertical)"
…underline captions	Control Panel → Folder Options → General tab → Click items as follows
Images, show as thumbnails in Explorer	Explorer → View → Thumbnails
…show in web pages	Control Panel → Internet Options → Advanced tab → Multimedia → Show pictures
…show placeholders in web pages (if pictures are disabled in web pages)	Control Panel → Internet Options → Advanced tab → Multimedia → Show image download placeholders
Indexing Service, enable/disable for individual drives	Explorer → right-click drive icon → Properties → General tab → Allow Indexing Service to index this disk for fast file searching
Insertion Point, change	Control Panel → Mouse → Pointers tab → choose "Text Select" from "Customize" list

Setting	Location
Install On Demand, enable/disable	Control Panel → Internet Options → Advanced tab → Browsing → Enable Install On Demand
Internet Call, default application	Control Panel → Internet Options → Programs tab → Internet Call
Internet Connection Firewall, enable/disable	Control Panel → Network Connections → right-click connection → Properties → Advanced tab → Protect my computer and network by limiting or preventing access to this computer from the Internet
...logging	Control Panel → Network Connections → right-click connection → Properties → Advanced tab → Settings → Security Logging tab
...settings	Control Panel → Network Connections → right-click connection → Properties → Advanced tab → Settings
Internet Connection, set up	Control Panel → Internet Options → Connection tab → Setup
Internet Explorer, abbreviate link addresses in status bar	Control Panel → Internet Options → Advanced tab → Browsing → Show friendly URLs
...ActiveX settings	Control Panel → Internet Options → Security tab → Custom Level
...additional security policies	Group Policy (*gpedit.msc*) → Computer Configuration → Administrative Templates → Windows Components → Internet Explorer Group Policy (*gpedit.msc*) → User Configuration → Administrative Templates → Windows Components → Internet Explorer
...animated GIFs (enable/disable)	Control Panel → Internet Options → Advanced tab → Multimedia → Play animations in web pages
...AutoComplete settings	See "AutoComplete"
...automatically check for updates	Control Panel → Internet Options → Advanced tab → Browsing → Automatically check for Internet Explorer updates
...automatically download linked pages for Desktop web pages	Control Panel → Display → Desktop tab → Customize Desktop → Web tab → select item → Properties → Download tab
...automatically update Desktop web pages	Control Panel → Display → Desktop tab → Customize Desktop → Web tab → select item → Properties → Schedule tab

Setting	Location
...buttons & controls, use display settings	Control Panel → Internet Options → Advanced tab → Browsing → Enable visual styles on buttons and controls in web pages
...cache settings	Control Panel → Internet Options → General tab → Temporary Internet Files section → Settings
...cache settings for encrypted pages	Control Panel → Internet Options → Advanced tab → Security → Do not save encrypted pages to disk
...cache, clear automatically when browser is closed	Control Panel → Internet Options → Advanced tab → Security → Empty Temporary Internet Files folder when browser is closed
...certificates for secure sites	See "Certificates"
...check to see if it is the default browser	Control Panel → Internet Options → Programs tab → Internet Explorer should check to see whether it is the default browser
...colors & fonts	Control Panel → Internet Options → General tab
...cookies	See "Cookies"
...default home page	Control Panel → Internet Options → General tab → Home page
...Desktop icon	Control Panel → Display → Desktop tab → Customize Desktop
...disable compositing effects when using Terminal Server	Control Panel → Internet Options → Advanced tab → Browsing → Force offscreen compositing even under Terminal Server
...download complete notification	Control Panel → Internet Options → Advanced tab → Browsing → Notify when downloads complete
...enable/disable HTTP 1.1	Control Panel → Internet Options → Advanced tab → HTTP 1.1 settings
...enable/disable moving or resizing web page items on Desktop	Control Panel → Display → Desktop tab → Customize Desktop → Web tab → Lock Desktop items
...enlarge picture boxes to accommodate "ALT" captions (if pictures are disabled in web pages)	Control Panel → Internet Options → Advanced tab → Accessibility → Always expand ALT text for images
...explain server error messages	Control Panel → Internet Options → Advanced tab → Browsing → Show friendly HTTP error messages

Setting	Location
…fading animation when moving from one web page to another	Control Panel → Internet Options → Advanced tab → Browsing → Enable page transitions
…Go button	See "Go button"
…hand icon (change)	Control Panel → Mouse → Pointers tab → choose "Link Select" from "Customize" list
…hide infrequently used Favorites	Control Panel → Internet Options → Advanced tab → Browsing → Enable Personalized Favorites Menu
…History settings	Control Panel → Internet Options → General tab → History section
…icon, change	Control Panel → Display → Desktop tab → Customize Desktop → General tab → select icon → Change Icon
…show on Desktop	Control Panel → Display → Desktop tab → Customize Desktop → General tab → Internet Explorer
…image placeholders (if pictures are disabled in web pages)	Control Panel → Internet Options → Advanced tab → Multimedia → Show image download placeholders
…Image Toolbar (enable/ disable)	Control Panel → Internet Options → Advanced tab → Multimedia → Enable Image Toolbar
…Link underline	Control Panel → Internet Options → Advanced tab → Browsing → Underline links
…list additional settings	System Information (*winmsd.exe*) → Internet Settings → Internet Explorer
…Media Bar content	Control Panel → Internet Options → Advanced tab → Multimedia → Don't display online media content in the media bar
…navigation keys	TweakUI → Explorer → Command Keys
…plugins (enable/disable)	Control Panel → Internet Options → Advanced tab → Browsing → Enable third-party browser extensions
…print background colors and images when printing web pages	Control Panel → Internet Options → Advanced tab → Printings → Print background colors and images
…profile assistant (enable/ disable)	Control Panel → Internet Options → Advanced tab → Security → Enable Profile Assistant
…restrict certain sites	Control Panel → Internet Options → Content tab → Content Advisor section

Setting	Location
…reuse folder windows when launching shortcuts	Control Panel → Internet Options → Advanced tab → Browsing → Reuse windows for launching shortcuts
…save form data	Control Panel → Internet Options → Content tab → AutoComplete
…saved web pages, link to image folder	TweakUI → Explorer → Manipulate connected files as a unit
…link to image folder	Control Panel → Folder Options → View tab → Managing pairs of Web pages and folders
…script, debugging	Control Panel → Internet Options → Advanced tab → Browsing → Disable script debugging
…error notification	Control Panel → Internet Options → Advanced tab → Browsing → Display a notification about every script error
…search, choose prefixes	TweakUI → Internet Explorer → Search
…from the address bar	Control Panel → Internet Options → Advanced tab → Search from the Address bar
…use classic	TweakUI → Explorer → Use Classic Search in Internet Explorer
…show web page on Desktop	Control Panel → Display → Desktop tab → Customize Desktop → Web tab
…shrink large images to fit browser window	Control Panel → Internet Options → Advanced tab → Multimedia → Enable Automatic Image Resizing
…smooth scrolling	Control Panel → Internet Options → Advanced tab → Browsing → Use smooth scrolling
…sounds (enable/disable)	Control Panel → Internet Options → Advanced tab → Multimedia → Play sounds in web pages
…SSL settings	Control Panel → Internet Options → Advanced tab → Security
…status bar shows abbreviated link addresses	Control Panel → Internet Options → Advanced tab → Browsing → Show friendly URLs
…toolbar background	TweakUI → Internet Explorer
…underline links	Control Panel → Internet Options → Advanced tab → Browsing → Underline links
…use passive mode in FTP	Control Panel → Internet Options → Advanced tab → Browsing → Use Passive FTP

Setting	Location
...video clips (enable/disable)	Control Panel → Internet Options → Advanced tab → Multimedia → Play videos in web pages
...view source, choose program	TweakUI → Internet Explorer → View Source
...warning for redirected form submission	Control Panel → Internet Options → Advanced tab → Security → Warn if forms submittal is being redirected
...warnings, enable/disable	Control Panel → Internet Options → Security tab → Custom Level
Internet icon, show in Start Menu (XP Start Menu only)	Control Panel → Taskbar and Start Menu → Start Menu tab → Customize → General tab → Internet
Internet Shortcuts, use same folder window or Explorer window to open web page	Control Panel → Internet Options → Advanced tab → Browsing → Reuse windows for launching shortcuts
Java, compile applets before running using the JIT (Just In Time) compiler	Control Panel → Internet Options → Advanced tab → Microsoft VM → JIT compiler for virtual machine enabled
...console	Control Panel → Internet Options → Advanced tab → Microsoft VM → Java console enabled
...logging	Control Panel → Internet Options → Advanced tab → Microsoft VM → Java logging enabled
...security settings	Control Panel → Internet Options → Security tab → Custom Level
Joystick settings	Control Panel → Game Controllers
Keyboard, choose international layout	Control Panel → Regional and Language Options → Language tab → Details
...enable alternative device	Control Panel → Accessibility Options → General tab → Use Serial Keys
...ignore brief or repeated keystrokes	Control Panel → Accessibility Options → Keyboard tab → Use FilterKeys
...specify type	Control Panel → Keyboard → Hardware tab → Properties → Driver tab → Update Driver → Install from a list of specific location → Next → Don't search → Next
...speed (repeat rate and delay)	Control Panel → Keyboard → Speed tab → Character repeat section
...Windows logo key combinations (enable/disable)	TweakUI → Explorer → Enable Windows+X hotkeys

Setting	Location
Keyboard shortcuts, hide until Alt key is pressed	Control Panel → Display → Appearance tab → Effects → Hide underlined letters for keyboard navigation until I press the Alt key
...show in menus and windows	Control Panel → Accessibility Options → Keyboard tab → Show extra keyboard help in programs
Language, settings for non-Unicode applications	Control Panel → Regional and Language Options → Advanced tab → Language for non-Unicode programs
...settings for text entry	Control Panel → Regional and Language Options → Language tab → Details
...settings in web pages	Control Panel → Internet Options → General tab → Languages
...use more than one	Control Panel → Regional and Language Options → Language tab → Details → Settings tab → Add
Listboxes, enable/disable animation	Control Panel → System → Advanced tab → Performance section → Settings → Visual Effects tab → Custom
Log off, show in Ctrl-Alt-Del window	Group Policy (*gpedit.msc*) → User Configuration → Administrative Templates → System → Ctrl+Alt+Del Options
...show in Start Menu (Classic Start Menu only)	Control Panel → Taskbar and Start Menu → Start Menu tab → Customize → "Advanced Start menu options" section → Display Log Off TweakUI → Explorer → Allow Logoff on Start Menu
Log on, automatic log on	TweakUI → Logon
...parse Autoexec.bat	TweakUI → Logon
...scripts policies	Group Policy (*gpedit.msc*) → Computer Configuration → Administrative Templates → System → Scripts Group Policy (*gpedit.msc*) → User Configuration → Administrative Templates → System → Scripts
...security policies	Group Policy (*gpedit.msc*) → Computer Configuration → Windows Settings → Security Settings → Local Policies → Security Options Group Policy (*gpedit.msc*) → Computer Configuration → Administrative Templates → System → Logon Group Policy (*gpedit.msc*) → User Configuration → Administrative Templates → System → Logon

Setting	Location
...use Welcome screen	Control Panel → User Accounts → Change the way users log on or off → Use the Welcome screen
Magnifier, move with focus change in web pages	Control Panel → Internet Options → Advanced tab → Accessibility → Move system caret with focus/selection changes
Mail Server, restrictions	Control Panel → Network Connections → right-click connection → Properties → Advanced tab → Settings → Services tab
Memory, priorities	Control Panel → System → Advanced tab → Performance section → Settings → Advanced tab → Memory usage section
...show amount of memory installed on display adapter	Control Panel → Display → Settings tab → Advanced → Adapter tab → Adapter Information section
...show amount of system memory installed	Control Panel → System → General tab
...virtual	See "Virtual Memory"
Menus, animation (enable/disable)	Control Panel → Display → Appearance tab → Effects → Use the following transition effect for menus and tooltips TweakUI → General → Enable menu animation Control Panel → System → Advanced tab → Performance section → Settings → Visual Effects tab → Custom
Menus, fading (enable/disable)	TweakUI → General → Enable menu fading
...fonts & colors	Control Panel → Display → Appearance tab → Advanced → Item list → choose "Menu"
...highlight color & font	Control Panel → Display → Appearance tab → Advanced → Item list → choose "Selected Items"
...shadows (enable/disable)	Control Panel → Display → Appearance tab → Effects → Show shadows under menus
...size	Control Panel → Display → Appearance tab → Advanced → Item list → choose "Menu"
...speed	TweakUI → Mouse
...underlined keyboard shortcuts (show/hide)	Control Panel → Display → Appearance tab → Effects → Hide underlined letters for keyboard navigation until I press the Alt key

Setting	Location
Message boxes, font	Control Panel → Display → Appearance tab → Advanced → Item list → choose "Message Box"
...sound	Control Panel → Sounds and Audio Devices → Sounds tab
...text color	Control Panel → Display → Appearance tab → Advanced → Item list → choose "Window"
Modems, settings	Control Panel → Phone and Modem Options → Modems tab
Mouse, auto-raise windows	TweakUI → Mouse → X-Mouse
...control with keyboard	Control Panel → Accessibility Options → Mouse tab
...detect accidental double-clicks	TweakUI → Explorer → Detect accidental double-clicks
...double-click speed	Control Panel → Mouse → Buttons tab → Double-click speed section
...double-click sensitivity	TweakUI → Mouse
...drag-drop sensitivity	TweakUI → Mouse
...drag without holding down buttons	Control Panel → Mouse → Buttons tab → ClickLock section
...enable alternative device	Control Panel → Accessibility Options → General tab → Use Serial Keys
...hide when typing	Control Panel → Mouse → Pointer Options tab → Hide pointer while typing
...hot tracking effects	TweakUI → General → Enable mouse hot tracking effects
...hot tracking effects color	TweakUI → Explorer → Colors
...hover sensitivity	TweakUI → Mouse → Hover
...lefthanded use	Control Panel → Mouse → Buttons tab → Switch primary and secondary buttons
...move to default button when window is opened	Control Panel → Mouse → Pointer Options tab → Automatically move pointer to the default button in a dialog box
...pointer	Control Panel → Mouse → Pointers tab
...precise control enhancement	Control Panel → Mouse → Pointer Options tab → Enhance pointer precision
...sensitivity	TweakUI → Mouse

Setting	Location
...shadow	Control Panel → Mouse → Pointers tab → Enable pointer shadow TweakUI → General → Enable cursor shadow
...show location with animated circles when Ctrl is pressed	Control Panel → Mouse → Pointer Options tab → Show location of pointer when I press the Ctrl key
...specify type	Control Panel → Mouse → Hardware tab → Properties → Driver tab → Update Driver → Install from a list of specific location → Next → Don't search → Next
...speed	Control Panel → Mouse → Pointer Options tab → Motion section
...switch left and right buttons	Control Panel → Mouse → Buttons tab → Switch primary and secondary buttons
...trails	Control Panel → Mouse → Pointer Options tab → Display pointer trails
...wheel, use for scrolling	TweakUI → Mouse → Wheel
My Computer, change icon	Control Panel → Display → Desktop tab → Customize Desktop → General tab → select icon → Change Icon
...show Control Panel	Control Panel → Folder Options → View tab → Show Control Panel in My Computer
...show first on Desktop	TweakUI → Desktop → First Icon
...show icon on Desktop	Control Panel → Display → Desktop tab → Customize Desktop → General tab → My Computer
...show in Start Menu (XP Start Menu only)	Control Panel → Taskbar and Start Menu → Start Menu tab → Customize → Advanced tab → "Start menu items" section → My Computer
My Documents, change icon	Control Panel → Display → Desktop tab → Customize Desktop → General tab → select icon → Change Icon
...clear recently opened documents from Start Menu (Classic Start Menu only)	Control Panel → Taskbar and Start Menu → Start Menu tab → Customize → Clear
...clear recently opened documents from Start Menu (XP Start Menu only)	Control Panel → Taskbar and Start Menu → Start Menu tab → Customize → Advanced tab → Clear List
...folder location	TweakUI → My Computer → Special Folders

Setting	Location
...show as menu in Start Menu (XP Start Menu only)	Control Panel → Taskbar and Start Menu → Start Menu tab → Customize → Advanced tab → "Start menu items" section → Expand My Documents
...show first on Desktop	TweakUI → Desktop → First Icon
...show icon on Desktop	Control Panel → Display → Desktop tab → Customize Desktop → General tab → My Documents
...show in Start Menu (Classic Start Menu only)	Control Panel → Taskbar and Start Menu → Start Menu tab → Customize → "Advanced Start menu options" section → My Documents
...show recently opened on Start Menu (XP Start Menu only)	Control Panel → Taskbar and Start Menu → Start Menu tab → Customize → Advanced tab → "Recent documents" section
My Music, repair folder	TweakUI → Repair
...show as menu Start Menu (XP Start Menu only)	Control Panel → Taskbar and Start Menu → Start Menu tab → Customize → Advanced tab → "Start menu items" section → My Music
My Network Places, history (enable/disable)	TweakUI → Explorer → Maintain network history
...icon, change	Control Panel → Display → Desktop tab → Customize Desktop → General tab → select icon → Change Icon
...icon, show on Desktop	Control Panel → Display → Desktop tab → Customize Desktop → General tab → My Network Places
...show in Start Menu (XP Start Menu only)	Control Panel → Taskbar and Start Menu → Start Menu tab → Customize → Advanced tab → "Start menu items" section → My Network Places
...View workgroup computers in common task pane (show/hide)	TweakUI → Explorer → Show "View workgroup computers" in Net Places
My Pictures, folder location	TweakUI → My Computer → Special Folders
...repair folder	TweakUI → Repair
...show as menu in Start Menu (Classic Start Menu only)	Control Panel → Taskbar and Start Menu → Start Menu tab → Customize → "Advanced Start menu options" section → Expand My Pictures
...show in Start Menu (Classic Start Menu only)	TweakUI → Explorer → Show My Pictures on classic Start Menu

Setting	Location
...show in Start Menu (XP Start Menu only)	Control Panel → Taskbar and Start Menu → Start Menu tab → Customize → Advanced tab → "Start menu items" section → My Pictures
My Videos, repair folder	TweakUI → Repair
Navigation keys on special keyboards, customize	TweakUI → Explorer → Command Keys
NetMeeting, make the default for Internet Calls	Control Panel → Internet Options → Programs tab → Internet Call
Network, add new connection	Control Panel → Network Connections → New Connection Wizard
...advanced adapter settings	Device Manager → right-click adapter → Properties → Advanced tab
...Authentication	Control Panel → Network Connections → right-click connection → Properties → Authentication tab
...bindings	Control Panel → Network Connections → Advanced → Advanced Settings → Adapters and Bindings tab Control Panel → Network Connections → right-click connection → Properties → General tab → turn on or off listed protocols and services
...bridge two connections	Control Panel → Network Connections → select two connections → Advanced → Network Bridge
...computer description	Control Panel → System → Computer Name tab
...computer name	Control Panel → System → Computer Name tab → Change
...connect to shared printer	Control Panel → Printers and Faxes → Add Printer → Next → A network printer, or a printer attached to another computer
...connection status	Control Panel → Network Connections → double-click connection → General tab
...disconnect mapped network drive	Explorer → Tools → Disconnect Network Drive
...DNS settings	Control Panel → Network Connections → right-click connection → Properties → General tab → Internet Protocol (TCP/IP) → Properties → Advanced → DNS tab

Setting	Location
...enable/disable	Control Panel → Network Connections → right-click connection → Enable or Disable
...Firewall	See "Internet Connection Firewall"
...include in Files or Folders search	Control Panel → Folder Options → View tab → Automatically search for network folders and printers
...install a network protocol or service	Control Panel → Network Connections → right-click connection → Properties → General tab → Install
...IP address and other connection information	Control Panel → Network Connections → double-click connection → Support tab
...join a Windows NT domain	Control Panel → System → Computer Name tab → Change
...map network drive	Explorer → Tools → Map Network Drive
...preliminary setup	Control Panel → Network Connections → Network Setup Wizard
...priorities	Control Panel → Network Connections → Advanced → Advanced Settings → Provider Order tab
...protocol, enable or disable for a connection	Control Panel → Network Connections → right-click connection → Properties → General tab → check or uncheck entries in list
...security policies	Group Policy (*gpedit.msc*) → Computer Configuration → Windows Settings → Security Settings → Local Policies → Security Options Group Policy (*gpedit.msc*) → Computer Configuration → Administrative Templates → Network Group Policy (*gpedit.msc*) → User Configuration → Administrative Templates → Network
...set IP address	Control Panel → Network Connections → right-click connection → Properties → General tab → Internet Protocol (TCP/IP) → Properties → Use the following IP address
...set multiple IP addresses	Control Panel → Network Connections → right-click connection → Properties → General tab → Internet Protocol (TCP/IP) → Properties → Advanced → IP Settings tab
...share printer	Control Panel → Printers and Faxes → right-click printer → Sharing → Shared as

Setting	Location
...show icon in taskbar notification area when connected	Control Panel → Network Connections → right-click connection → Properties → General tab → Show icon in notification area when connected
...SNMP components (install/uninstall)	Control Panel → Network Connections → Advanced → Optional Networking Components → Management and Monitoring Tools
...TCP/IP filtering	Control Panel → Network Connections → right-click connection → Properties → General tab → Internet Protocol (TCP/IP) → Properties → Advanced → Options tab → TCP/IP filtering → Properties
...TCP/IP settings	Control Panel → Network Connections → right-click connection → Properties → General tab → Internet Protocol (TCP/IP) → Properties
...uninstall a protocol or service	Control Panel → Network Connections → right-click connection → Properties → General tab → Uninstall
...WINS settings	Control Panel → Network Connections → right-click connection → Properties → General tab → Internet Protocol (TCP/IP) → Properties → Advanced → WINS tab
Network Connections, automatically dial	Control Panel → Internet Options → Connection tab
...security policies	Group Policy (*gpedit.msc*) → User Configuration → Administrative Templates → Network → Network Connections
...show as menu in Start Menu (Classic Start Menu only)	Control Panel → Taskbar and Start Menu → Start Menu tab → Customize → "Advanced Start menu options" section → Expand Network Connections
...show in Start Menu (Classic Start Menu only)	TweakUI → Explorer → Show Network Connections on classic Start Menu
...show in Start Menu (XP Start Menu only)	Control Panel → Taskbar and Start Menu → Start Menu tab → Customize → Advanced tab → "Start menu items" section → Network Connections
Newsgroup reader, default	Control Panel → Internet Options → Programs tab → Newsgroups
Notification Area	See "Taskbar Notification Area"
Numbers, customize display	Control Panel → Regional and Language Options → Regional Options tab → Customize → Numbers tab

Setting	Location
ODBC data sources, restrict access	Control Panel → Internet Options → Security tab → Custom Level
Offline Files, action to take when network connection is lost	Control Panel → Folder Options → Offline Files tab → Advanced
…automatic synchronization	Explorer → Tools → Synchronize → Setup → Logon/ Lofoff tab → Automatically synchronize the selected items…
…automatic synchronization on idle	Explorer → Tools → Synchronize → Setup → On Idle tab → Advanced
…compatibility with computers running on batteries	Explorer → Tools → Synchronize → Setup → On Idle tab → Advanced → Prevent synchronization when my computer is running on battery power
…enable scheduling of Desktop web page updates	Control Panel → Internet Options → Advanced tab → Browsing → Enable offline items to be synchronized on a schedule
…security policies	Group Policy (*gpedit.msc*) → User Configuration → Administrative Templates → Network → Offline Files
…settings	Control Panel → Folder Options → Offline Files tab Explorer → Tools → Synchronize → Setup
…synchronize	Explorer → Tools → Synchronize
Outlook Express, make the default	Control Panel → Internet Options → Programs tab → E-mail or Newsgroups
…repair unread mail count	TweakUI → Repair
Parental Control of web sites	Control Panel → Internet Options → Content tab → Content Advisor section
Passwords, automatic logon	Control Panel → Internet Options → Security tab → Custom Level → User Authentication
…change	Control Panel → User Accounts → select an account → Change my password
…expiration	Group Policy (*gpedit.msc*) → Computer Configuration → Windows Settings → Security Settings → Account Policies → Password Policy
…prevent forgotten passwords	Control Panel → User Accounts → select an account → Related Tasks section → Prevent a forgotten password

Setting	Location
...require for exiting screen saver	Control Panel → Display → Screen Saver tab → On resume, password protect
...require for resuming from standby mode	Control Panel → Power Options → Advanced tab → Prompt for password when computer resumes from standby
...saving in web pages	Control Panel → Internet Options → Content tab → AutoComplete
...security policies	Group Policy (*gpedit.msc*) → Computer Configuration → Windows Settings → Security Settings → Account Policies → Password Policy
...show "Change Password" in Ctrl-Alt-Del window	Group Policy (*gpedit.msc*) → User Configuration → Administrative Templates → System → Ctrl+Alt+Del Options
Path, show full path in folder windows	Control Panel → Folder Options → View tab → Display the full path in the title bar/Display the full path in the address bar
Personalized menus, Favorites	Control Panel → Internet Options → Advanced tab → Browsing → Enable Personalized Favorites Menu
Pictures	See "Images"
Places bar, customize	TweakUI → Common Dialogs
Pointer	See "Mouse"
Pop-up help windows	See "Tooltips"
Power Management	See "Advanced Power Management"
Print Server settings	Control Panel → Printers and Faxes → File → Server Properties
Printers, advanced settings	Group Policy (*gpedit.msc*) → Computer Configuration → Administrative Templates → Printers Group Policy (*gpedit.msc*) → User Configuration → Administrative Templates → Printers
...cancel printing of all documents	Control Panel → Printers and Faxes → right-click printer → Cancel All Documents
...cancel printing of one document	Control Panel → Printers and Faxes → double-click printer → right-click document → Cancel
...change settings for a single application	Open application → File → Print or Printer Setup

Setting	Location
…change settings for all applications	Control Panel → Printers and Faxes → right-click printer → Properties
…connect to a printer on your network	Control Panel → Printers and Faxes → Add Printer → Next → A network printer, or a printer attached to another computer
…install	Control Panel → Printers and Faxes → Add Printer
…pause printing	Control Panel → Printers and Faxes → right-click printer → Pause Printing
…print background colors and images when printing web pages	Control Panel → Internet Options → Advanced tab → Printings → Print background colors and images
…set default printer	Control Panel → Printers and Faxes → right-click printer → Set as Default Printer
…share with other computers on network	Control Panel → Printers and Faxes → right-click printer → Sharing → Shared as
…show as menu in Start Menu (Classic Start Menu only)	Control Panel → Taskbar and Start Menu → Start Menu tab → Customize → "Advanced Start menu options" section → Expand Printers
…show in Start Menu (XP Start Menu only)	Control Panel → Taskbar and Start Menu → Start Menu tab → Customize → Advanced tab → "Start menu items" section → Printers and Faxes
…uninstall	Control Panel → Printers and Faxes → right-click printer → Delete
…view status	Control Panel → Printers and Faxes → double-click printer
Processor, priorities	Control Panel → System → Advanced tab → Performance section → Settings → Advanced tab → Processor scheduling section
…show details	Control Panel → System → General tab
Profile Assistant, enable/disable	Control Panel → Internet Options → Advanced tab → Security → Enable Profile Assistant
Proxy settings	Control Panel → Internet Options → Connection tab → LAN Settings
Quick Launch toolbar, show on Taskbar	Control Panel → Taskbar and Start Menu → Taskbar tab → Show Quick Launch Right-click on taskbar → Toolbars → Quick Launch
Recent Documents	See "Documents"

Setting	Location
Recycle Bin, Desktop icon	Control Panel → Display → Desktop tab → Customize Desktop
Registered User, view	Control Panel → System → General tab
Registry Editor, repair	TweakUI → Repair
Remote Assistance, allow invitations to be sent	Control Panel → System → Remote tab → Remote Assistance tab
Remote Desktop, enable incoming connections	Control Panel → System → Remote tab → Remote Desktop tab
Report crashes to Microsoft	Control Panel → System → Advanced tab → Error Reporting
Run, show in Start Menu (Classic Start Menu only)	Control Panel → Taskbar and Start Menu → Start Menu tab → Customize → "Advanced Start menu options" section → Display Run
...show in Start Menu (XP Start Menu only)	Control Panel → Taskbar and Start Menu → Start Menu tab → Customize → Advanced tab → "Start menu items" section → Run Command
Scheduled Tasks, add a task	Control Panel → Scheduled Tasks → Add Scheduled Task
...choose user for a single task	Control Panel → Scheduled Tasks → right-click task → Properties → Task tab → Run as
...choose user for AT service	Control Panel → Scheduled Tasks → Advanced → AT Service Account
...compatibility with computers running on batteries	Control Panel → Scheduled Tasks → right-click task → Properties → Settings tab → Power Management section
...delete a task	Control Panel → Scheduled Tasks → right-click task → Delete
...delete completed tasks automatically	Control Panel → Scheduled Tasks → right-click task → Properties → Settings tab → Delete the task if it is not scheduled to run again
...enable/disable	Control Panel → Scheduled Tasks → Advanced → Stop Using Task Scheduler or Start Using Task Scheduler
...enable/disable a single task	Control Panel → Scheduled Tasks → right-click task → Properties → Task tab → Enabled
...log	Control Panel → Scheduled Tasks → Advanced → View Log

Setting	Location
…missed task notification	Control Panel → Scheduled Tasks → Advanced → Notify Me of Missed Tasks
…pause	Control Panel → Scheduled Tasks → Advanced → Pause Task Scheduler
…perform only if computer is idle	Control Panel → Scheduled Tasks → right-click task → Properties → Settings tab → Idle Time section
…repeat settings for a single task	Control Panel → Scheduled Tasks → right-click task → Properties → Schedule tab → Advanced
…schedule settings for a single task	Control Panel → Scheduled Tasks → right-click task → Properties → Schedule tab
…security policies	Group Policy (*gpedit.msc*) → Computer Configuration → Administrative Templates → Windows Components → Task Scheduler Group Policy (*gpedit.msc*) → User Configuration → Administrative Templates → Windows Components → Task Scheduler
…stop hung tasks	Control Panel → Scheduled Tasks → right-click task → Properties → Settings tab → Stop the task if it runs for…
Screen	See "Display"
Screen Saver settings	Control Panel → Display → Screen Saver tab
Scrollbars, color	Control Panel → Display → Appearance tab → Advanced → Item list → choose "3d Objects"
…size	Control Panel → Display → Appearance tab → Advanced → Item list → choose "Scrollbar"
Search, address bar	Control Panel → Internet Options → Advanced tab → Search from the Address bar
…classic search in Explorer	TweakUI → Explorer → Use Classic Search in Explorer
…customize navigation key	TweakUI → Explorer → Command Keys
…include network folders and printers	Control Panel → Folder Options → View tab → Automatically search for network folders and printers
Send To, folder location	TweakUI → My Computer → Special Folders
Setup, location of setup files	TweakUI → My Computer → Special Folders → Installation Path
Shared folders, include in searches	Control Panel → Folder Options → View tab → Automatically search for network folders and printers

Setting	Location
...make accessible to all users	Control Panel → Folder Options → View tab → Use simple file sharing
Shift Key, make it "sticky"	Control Panel → Accessibility Options → Keyboard tab → Use StickyKeys
Shortcuts, overlay icon	TweakUI → Explorer → Shortcut
...show "Shortcut to" prefix	TweakUI → Explorer → Prefix "Shortcut to" on new shortcuts
Single-click required to open icons	Control Panel → Folder Options → General tab → Single-click to open an item
Software, install or uninstall	Control Panel → Add or Remove Programs
...install or uninstall (network components)	Control Panel → Network Connections → Advanced → Optional Networking Components
...installation security policies	Group Policy (*gpedit.msc*) → Computer Configuration → Administrative Templates → Windows Components → Windows Installer Group Policy (*gpedit.msc*) → User Configuration → Administrative Templates → Windows Components → Windows Installer
Sounds, beep on errors	TweakUI → General → Beep on errors
...default audio devices for playback, recording, and MIDI	Control Panel → Sounds and Audio Devices → Audio tab
...disable unwanted audio devices	Control Panel → Sounds and Audio Devices → Audio tab → Use only default devices
...events that trigger sounds	Control Panel → Sounds and Audio Devices → Sounds tab
...list devices	Control Panel → Sounds and Audio Devices → Hardware tab
...mute all	Control Panel → Sounds and Audio Devices → Volume tab → Mute
...navigation keys on special keyboards	TweakUI → Explorer → Command Keys
...play in web pages	Control Panel → Internet Options → Advanced tab → Multimedia → Play sounds in web pages
...play sounds when Caps Lock, Num Lock, or Scroll Lock is pressed	Control Panel → Accessibility Options → Keyboard tab → Use ToggleKeys

Setting	Location
...show visual notification	Control Panel → Accessibility Options → Sound tab
...speaker, enable/disable PC speaker	TweakUI → General → Beep on errors
...speaker orientation	Control Panel → Sounds and Audio Devices → Volume tab → Speaker settings section → Advanced → Speakers tab
...speaker troubleshooting	Control Panel → Sounds and Audio Devices → Volume tab → Speaker settings section → Advanced → Performance tab
...speaker volume	Control Panel → Sounds and Audio Devices → Volume tab → Speaker settings section → Speaker Volume
...surround sound setup	Control Panel → Sounds and Audio Devices → Volume tab → Speaker settings section → Advanced → Speakers tab
...volume	Control Panel → Sounds and Audio Devices → Volume tab
...volume from keyboard	TweakUI → Explorer → Command Keys
Speech, recording voice	See "Voice"
...select preferred audio device	Control Panel → Speech → Text to Speech tab → Audio Output
...speed	Control Panel → Speech → Text to Speech tab → Voice speed section
...voice selection	Control Panel → Speech → Text to Speech tab → Voice selection section
...volume	Volume Control (*sndvol32.exe*) → adjust master or "Wave" controls
Start Menu, button look and feel	Control Panel → Display → Appearance tab → Windows and buttons list
...clear list of recently opened applications	Control Panel → Taskbar and Start Menu → Start Menu tab → Customize → General tab → Clear List
...enable dragging and dropping (Classic Start Menu only)	Control Panel → Taskbar and Start Menu → Start Menu tab → Customize → "Advanced Start menu options" section → Enable Dragging and Dropping
...enable dragging and dropping (XP Start Menu only)	Control Panel → Taskbar and Start Menu → Start Menu tab → Customize → Advanced tab → "Start menu items" section → Enable Dragging and Dropping

Setting	Location
...folder location	TweakUI → My Computer → Special Folders
...Frequently Used Programs, ban items from list	TweakUI → Taskbar → XP Start Menu
...hide infrequently accessed applications (Classic Start Menu only)	Control Panel → Taskbar and Start Menu → Start Menu tab → Customize → "Advanced Start menu options" section → Use Personalized Menus
...highlight newly installed programs (XP Start Menu only)	Control Panel → Taskbar and Start Menu → Start Menu tab → Customize → Advanced tab → Highlight newly installed programs
...look and feel	Control Panel → Taskbar and Start Menu → Start Menu tab → "Start menu" or "Classic Start menu"
...number of recently opened applications to show (XP Start Menu only)	Control Panel → Taskbar and Start Menu → Start Menu tab → Customize → General tab → "Programs" section
...open menus when hovering with mouse (XP Start Menu only)	Control Panel → Taskbar and Start Menu → Start Menu tab → Customize → Advanced tab → Open submenus when I pause on them with my mouse
...size of icons (Classic Start Menu only)	Control Panel → Taskbar and Start Menu → Start Menu tab → Customize → Advanced tab → "Start menu items" section → Show Small Icons in Start Menu
...size of icons (XP Start Menu only)	Control Panel → Taskbar and Start Menu → Start Menu tab → Customize → General tab → "Select an icon size for programs" section
Startup, folder location	TweakUI → My Computer → Special Folders
...log	Control Panel → System → Advanced tab → Startup and Recovery section → Settings → System failure section
...multiboot menu settings	Control Panel → System → Advanced tab → Startup and Recovery section → Settings → System startup section
...sound	See "Sounds"
Status Bar, show in Explorer	Explorer → View → Status Bar
Stylesheets, impose a single stylesheet for all web pages	Control Panel → Internet Options → General tab → Accessibility → Format documents using my style sheet

Setting	Location
Style, apply to controls in web pages	Control Panel → Internet Options → Advanced tab → Browsing → Enable visual styles on buttons and controls in web pages
...enable/disable all styles	Control Panel → System → Advanced tab → Performance section → Settings → Visual Effects tab → Custom
...visual style of windows and buttons	Control Panel → Display → Appearance tab → Windows and buttons list
Swap File, size and location	See "Virtual Memory"
Synchronize	See "Offline Files"
System Restore, disk space usage	Control Panel → System → System Restore tab → Disk space usage section
...enable/disable	Control Panel → System → System Restore tab → Turn off System Restore
...policies	Group Policy (gpedit.msc) → Computer Configuration → Administrative Templates → System → System Restore
...status	Control Panel → System → System Restore tab → Status section
Task, show extra task pane in folder windows	Control Panel → Folder Options → General tab → Tasks section
Task Manager, show in Ctrl-Alt-Del window	Group Policy (gpedit.msc) → User Configuration → Administrative Templates → System → Ctrl+Alt+Del Options
Task Scheduler	See "Scheduled Tasks"
Taskbar, flash buttons	TweakUI → General → Focus
...group buttons by application	Control Panel → Taskbar and Start Menu → Taskbar tab → Group similar taskbar buttons
...group buttons by application (customize)	TweakUI → Taskbar → Grouping
...hide when not in use	Control Panel → Taskbar and Start Menu → Taskbar tab → Auto-hide the taskbar
...keep on top of other windows	Control Panel → Taskbar and Start Menu → Taskbar tab → Keep the taskbar on top of other windows
...move to a different screen location	Click on an empty portion of the taskbar and drag

Setting	Location
...prevent moving and resizing	Control Panel → Taskbar and Start Menu → Taskbar tab → Lock the taskbar Right-click on taskbar → Toolbars → Lock the taskbar
...resize	Drag the border of the taskbar to make it larger or smaller
...sliding button animation (enable/disable)	Control Panel → System → Advanced tab → Performance section → Settings → Visual Effects tab → Custom
...style	Control Panel → Display → Appearance tab → Windows and buttons list
Taskbar Notification Area, hide infrequently accessed applications	Control Panel → Taskbar and Start Menu → Taskbar tab → Hide inactive icons
...network icon	Control Panel → Network Connections → right-click connection → Properties → General tab → Show icon in notification area when connected
...power icon	Control Panel → Power Options → Advanced tab → Always show icon on the taskbar
...volume control (yellow speaker)	Control Panel → Sounds and Audio Devices → Volume tab → Place volume icon in the taskbar
Telephony settings	Control Panel → Phone and Modem Options → Advanced tab
Telnet Server, restrictions	Control Panel → Network Connections → right-click connection → Properties → Advanced tab → Settings → Services tab
Temporary Internet Files, clear automatically when browser is closed	Control Panel → Internet Options → Advanced tab → Security → Empty Temporary Internet Files folder when browser is closed
...policy regarding encrypted pages	Control Panel → Internet Options → Advanced tab → Security → Do not save encrypted pages to disk
...settings	Control Panel → Internet Options → General tab → Temporary Internet Files section → Settings
Terminal Server, disable compositing effects in Internet Explorer	Control Panel → Internet Options → Advanced tab → Browsing → Force offscreen compositing even under Terminal Server

Setting	Location
...security policies	Group Policy (*gpedit.msc*) → Computer Configuration → Administrative Templates → Windows Components → Terminal Services Group Policy (*gpedit.msc*) → User Configuration → Administrative Templates → Windows Components → Terminal Services
Text Cursor, blink rate	Control Panel → Keyboard → Speed tab → Cursor blink rate
...blink rate & size	Control Panel → Accessibility Options → Display tab → Cursor Options section
...change mouse "I-beam" cursor	Control Panel → Mouse → Pointers tab → choose "Text Select" from "Customize" list
Themes	Control Panel → Display → Themes tab
Thumbnails, cache (enable/disable)	Control Panel → Folder Options → View tab → Do not cache thumbnails
...image quality	TweakUI → Explorer → Thumbnails
...show in Explorer	Explorer → View → Thumbnails
...size	TweakUI → Explorer → Thumbnails
Time, customize display	Control Panel → Regional and Language Options → Regional Options tab → Customize → Time tab
...set	Control Panel → Date and Time → Date & Time tab
...synchronize with Internet time server automatically	Control Panel → Date and Time → Internet Time tab
...time service policies	Group Policy (*gpedit.msc*) → Computer Configuration → Administrative Templates → System → Windows Time Service
...time zone	Control Panel → Date and Time → Time Zone tab
Title bar, font, color, and size	Control Panel → Display → Appearance tab → Advanced → Item list → choose "Active Title Bar" or "Inactive Title Bar"
...size only	Control Panel → Display → Appearance tab → Advanced → Item list → choose "Caption Buttons"
Toolbar, size and font for floating toolbar captions	Control Panel → Display → Appearance tab → Advanced → Item list → choose "Palette Title"

Setting	Location
Tooltips, animation	Control Panel → Display → Appearance tab → Effects → Use the following transition effect for menus and tooltips TweakUI → General → Enable tooltip animation
...animation (enable/disable)	Control Panel → System → Advanced tab → Performance section → Settings → Visual Effects tab → Custom
...enable/disable (Desktop, taskbar, and Explorer only)	Control Panel → Folder Options → View tab → Show pop-up description for folder and Desktop items
...fade (enable/disable)	TweakUI → General → Enable tooltip fade
...font & color	Control Panel → Display → Appearance tab → Advanced → Item list → choose "ToolTip"
...big "balloon" tooltips that pop up from taskbar notification area	See "Balloon tips"
Transition effects, enable/disable	Control Panel → Display → Appearance tab → Effects → Use the following transition effect for menus and tooltips
Tray	See "Taskbar Notification Area"
Uninstall Hardware	Control Panel → Add Hardware
Uninstall Software	Control Panel → Add or Remove Programs
Uninterruptible Power Supply (UPS) settings	Control Panel → Power Options → UPS tab
Usernames in web pages, saving	Control Panel → Internet Options → Content tab → AutoComplete
Users, add new user account	Control Panel → User Accounts → Create a new account
...allow fast switching between users	Control Panel → User Accounts → Change the way users log on or off → Use Fast User Switching
...multiple profiles for each user account	Control Panel → System → Advanced tab → User Profiles section → Settings
...passwords	See "Passwords"
...registered user	See "Registered User"

Setting	Location
…security policies	Group Policy (*gpedit.msc*) → Computer Configuration → Windows Settings → Security Settings → Local Policies → User Rights Assignment
	Group Policy (*gpedit.msc*) → Computer Configuration → Administrative Templates → System → User Profiles
	Group Policy (*gpedit.msc*) → User Configuration → Administrative Templates → System → User Profiles
…security policies for groups	Group Policy (*gpedit.msc*) → Computer Configuration → Administrative Templates → System → Group Policy
	Group Policy (*gpedit.msc*) → User Configuration → Administrative Templates → System → Group Policy
Video, play in web pages	Control Panel → Internet Options → Advanced tab → Multimedia → Play videos in web pages
Virtual memory, settings	Control Panel → System → Advanced tab → Performance section → Settings → Advanced tab → Change
Voice, calibrate volume settings	Control Panel → Sounds and Audio Devices → Voice tab → Test hardware
…playback and recording volume	Control Panel → Sounds and Audio Devices → Voice tab
…speech synthesis	See "Speech"
Volume	See "Sounds"
Wallpaper	See "Background"
Warnings in web pages, enable/disable	Control Panel → Internet Options → Security tab → Custom Level
Web pages	See "Internet Explorer"
…set default browser	Control Panel → Internet Options → Programs tab → Internet Explorer should check to see whether it is the default browser
…set default editor	Control Panel → Internet Options → Programs tab → HTML Editor
Web Server, restrictions	Control Panel → Network Connections → right-click connection → Properties → Advanced tab → Settings → Services tab
Welcome screen, enable/disable	Control Panel → User Accounts → Change the way users log on or off → Use the Welcome screen

Setting	Location
Windows, background of MDI windows	Control Panel → Display → Appearance tab → Advanced → Item list → choose "Application Background"
...background of non-MDI windows	Control Panel → Display → Appearance tab → Advanced → Item list → choose "Window"
...cascade all open application windows	Right-click on taskbar → Cascade Windows
...closing crashed applications	Task Manager (*taskmgr.exe*) → Applications tab
...closing hidden applications	Task Manager (*taskmgr.exe*) → Processes tab
...color of borders	Control Panel → Display → Appearance tab → Advanced → Item list → choose "3d Objects"
...minimize all open application windows	⊞ + D
...minimize/maximize animation	TweakUI → General → Enable window animation
...show outline or full window when dragging	Control Panel → Display → Appearance tab → Effects → Show window contents while dragging
...tile all open application windows	Right-click on taskbar → Tile Windows Horizontally or Tile Windows Vertically
...title bar font, color, and size	Control Panel → Display → Appearance tab → Advanced → Item list → choose "Active Title Bar" or "Inactive Title Bar"
Windows Explorer, access digital camera memory as a drive (still camera only)	Control Panel → Scanners and Cameras → Add Device
...additional security policies	Group Policy (*gpedit.msc*) → User Configuration → Administrative Templates → Windows Components → Windows Explorer
...columns in details view	Explorer → View → Details → View → Choose Details
...group similar items	Explorer → View Arrange Icons by → Show in Groups
...refresh view	Explorer → View → Refresh or press F5
...reuse window when launching Internet shortcuts	Control Panel → Internet Options → Advanced tab → Browsing → Reuse windows for launching shortcuts

Setting	Location
...search	See "Search"
...show lines in tree view (Folders Explorer bar)	Control Panel → Folder Options → View tab → Display simple folder view in Explorer's Folders list
...show Status Bar	Explorer → View → Status Bar
...toolbar, background	TweakUI → Internet Explorer
...toolbar, customize	Explorer → View → Toolbars → Customize
...toolbar, icon size	Explorer → View → Toolbars → Customize → Icon options
...toolbar, prevent being moved	Explorer → View → Toolbars → Lock the Toolbars
...toolbar, text captions	Explorer → View → Toolbars → Customize → Text options
Windows File Protection, advanced settings	Group Policy (*gpedit.msc*) → Computer Configuration → Administrative Templates → System → Windows File Protection
Windows Media Player, change as default for CDs	TweakUI → My Computer → AutoPlay
Windows Registered User information	Control Panel → System → General tab
Windows Update	Internet Explorer → Tools → Windows Update
...automatic updating	Control Panel → System → Automatic Updates tab
Windows version	Control Panel → System → General tab
Windows XP Style for screen elements	Control Panel → Display → Appearance tab → Windows and buttons list

PART V

Registry Tweaks

The Registry is a database containing all the settings for Windows XP, as well as the applications installed on your system. All your file types are stored in the Registry, as well as all the network, hardware, and software settings for Windows XP and all the particular configuration options for most of the software you've installed.

Many advanced settings in Windows XP can only be changed by manipulating data in the Registry. The solutions in this chapter detail some of the more useful and frequently needed Registry tweaks.

Registry Editor Crash Course

Although the Registry is stored in multiple files on your hard disk, it is represented by a single logical hierarchical structure, similar to the folders on your hard disk. The Registry Editor (*Regedit.exe*) is included with Windows XP to enable you to view and manually edit the contents of the Registry.

When you open the Registry Editor, you'll see a window divided into two panes: the left side shows a tree with *keys* (represented as folders), and the right side shows the contents (*values*) stored in the currently selected key.

Editing the Registry generally involves navigating down through branches to a particular key and then modifying an existing value or creating a new key or value. You can modify the contents of any value by double-clicking it.

WARNING

Although most Registry settings are entirely benign, you can irrevocably disable certain components of Windows XP—or even prevent Windows from starting—if you don't excercise some caution. You can limit the risk by creating Registry patches (backups) of keys before you modify their contents by going to File → Export. Better yet, a complete system backup will ensure that even the most severe mistakes are recoverable.

To add a new key or value, select New from the Edit menu, select what you want to add, and then type a name. You can delete a key or value by clicking on it and pressing the Del key or by right-clicking on it and selecting Delete. You can also rename any existing value and *almost* any key with the same methods used to rename files in Explorer: right-click on an object and click Rename, click on it twice (slowly), or just highlight it and press the F2 key. Renaming a key or value is a safe alternative to deleting.

Similar to Explorer, though, is the notion of a *path*. A Registry path is a location in the Registry described by the series of nested keys in which a setting is located. For example, if a particular value is in the Microsoft key under SOFTWARE, which is under HKEY_LOCAL_MACHINE, the Registry path is HKEY_LOCAL_MACHINE\SOFTWARE\Microsoft.

Registry Structure

There are five primary, or "root," branches, each containing a specific portion of the information stored in the Registry:

HKEY_CLASSES_ROOT

This branch contains the information that comprises your Windows file types. This entire branch is a symbolic link, or "mirror," of HKEY_LOCAL_MACHINE\SOFTWARE\Classes, but is displayed separately in this branch for clarity and easy access.

HKEY_USERS

This branch contains a sub-branch for the currently logged-in user, the name of which is the current user's SID (security identifier), a unique, 37-digit string of numbers. Use HKEY_CURRENT_USER for a more convenient point of entry to the data in this branch.

HKEY_CURRENT_USER

This branch points to a portion of HKEY_USERS, signifying the currently logged-in user. This way, any application can read and write settings for the current user without having to know which user is currently logged on. In each user's branch are the settings for that user, such as Control Panel and Explorer settings, application preferences, and other personal settings.

The Software branch, subdivided by software manufacturer and application name, is where you'll find most of the interesting settings. As though Windows was just another application on your system, you'll find most user-specific Windows settings in HKEY_CURRENT_USER\ Software\Microsoft\Windows.

HKEY_LOCAL_MACHINE

This branch contains information about all the hardware and software installed on your computer that *isn't* specific to the currently logged-in user. The settings in this branch are the same for all users on your system. The Software branch, similar to the one in HKEY_CURRENT_USER, contains settings arranged by software manufacturer and then product name.

HKEY_CURRENT_CONFIG

This branch typically contains a small amount of information, most of which simply points to other portions of the Registry. There's little reason to mess with this branch.

Value Types

Values are where Registry data is actually stored (as opposed to keys, which are simply used to organize values). The Registry contains several types of values, each appropriate to the type of data it is intended to hold. There are five primary types of values that are displayed and modified in the Registry Editor:

String values (REG_SZ)

> String values contain *strings* of characters, more commonly known as plain text.

String array/Multi-String values (REG_MULTI_SZ)

> Contains several strings, concatenated (glued) together and separated by null characters. Although Registry Editor lets you create these values, it's impossible to type null characters (ASCII character #0) from the keyboard. The only way to generate a null character is programmatically or via cut-and-paste.

Expandable string values (REG_EXPAND_SZ)

> Contains special variables, into which Windows substitutes information before delivering to the owning application. For example, an expanded string value intended to point to a sound file may contain %SystemRoot%\Media\ doh.wav. When Windows reads this value from the Registry, it substitutes the full Windows path for the variable, %SystemRoot%; the resulting data then becomes (depending on where Windows is installed) c:\Windows\Media\ doh.wav. This way, the value data is correct regardless of the location of the Windows folder.

Binary values (REG_BINARY)

> Similarly to string values, binary values hold strings of characters. The difference is the way the data is entered. Instead of a standard text box, binary data is entered with hexadecimal codes in an interface commonly

known as a *hex editor*. Each individual character is specified by a two-digit number in base-16 (e.g., 6E is equivalent to 110 in base 10), which allows characters not found on the keyboard to be entered. You can type hex codes on the left or normal text on the right, depending on where you click with the mouse.

DWORD values (REG_DWORD)

Essentially, a DWORD is a number. Often, the contents of a DWORD value are easily understood, such as 0 for no and 1 for yes, or 60 for the number of seconds in some timeout setting. A DWORD value would be used where only numerical digits are allowed, whereas string and binary values allow anything.

In the DWORD value editor, you can change the base of the number displayed, a setting that will result in the wrong value being entered if set incorrectly. In most cases, you'll want to select Decimal (even though it's not the default), because decimal notation is what we use for ordinary counting numbers.

The application that creates each value in the Registry solely determines the particular type and purpose of the value. In other words, no strict rules limit which types are used in which circumstances or how values are named. A programmer may choose to store, say, the high scores for some game in a binary value called High Scores or in a string value called Lard Lad Donuts.

An important thing to notice at this point is the string value named (default) that appears at the top of every key. The default value cannot be removed or renamed, although its contents can be changed; an empty default value is signified by value not set. The (default) value doesn't necessarily have any special meaning that would differentiate it from any other value, apart from what might have been assigned by the programmer of the particular application that created the key. Figure 5 shows an example of such a value being edited.

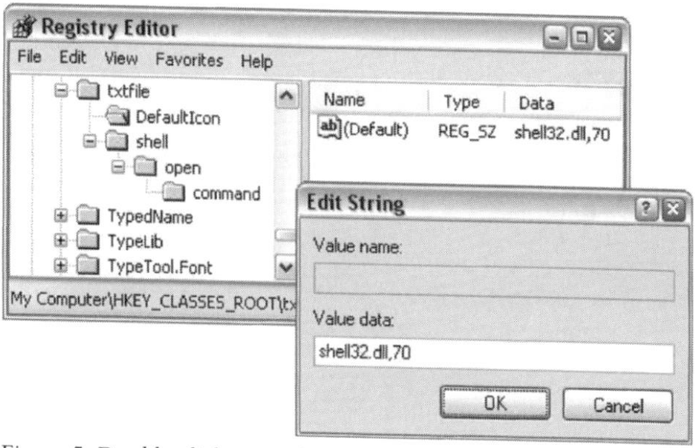

Figure 5. Double-click any value to edit its contents

Registry Tweaks

Each of the following tweaks points to a Registry path, and then describes the value (or values) that need to be modified. If any of the keys or values specified don't exist on your system, simply create them as directed. The topics covered include Files, Folders, and File Types (next), Performance Tweaks, and User Account and Network Settings.

Files, Folders, and File Types

These next few settings deal with file types, which affect files, folders, Desktop icons, and other objects.

Add Delete and Rename to the Recycle Bin's context menu

Location

    HKEY_CLASSES_ROOT\CLSID\{645FF040-5081-101B-9F08-
    00AA002F954E}\ShellFolder\

Directions

Set the Attributes value to 70 01 00 20 for Delete and Rename, or 50 01 00 20 for Rename only (the default is 40 01 00 20). Then, right-click the Recycle Bin and select Rename or Delete.

Hide all Desktop icons

Location

HKEY_CURRENT_USER\Software\Microsoft\Windows\
CurrentVersion\Policies\Explorer

Directions

Create a binary value called NoDesktop and set it to 01 00 00 00 to hide all Desktop icons. Delete the NoDesktop value to restore the Desktop icons.

Redirect the My Computer icon

Location

HKEY_CLASSES_ROOT\CLSID\{20D04FE03AEA-1069-A2D8-08002B30309D}\shell

Directions

Set the (Default) value to Open. Then, create a key named Open, and then another named Command (inside Open). Set the (Default) value to the command line to launch (such as \Windows\Explorer.exe).

Get rid of the Shared Documents folder

Location

HKEY_LOCAL_MACHINE\SOFTWARE\Microsoft\Windows\
CurrentVersion\Explorer\MyComputer\NameSpace\
DelegateFolders

Directions

Under this branch, you should see several subkeys, each named for a different Class ID. Delete the one named {59031a47-3f72-44a7-89c5-5595fe6b30ee}.

Remove an entry from Explorer's New menu

Location

> HKEY_CLASSES_ROOT\\{some file type key}

Directions

> Delete the ShellNew key under any file type key to remove that file type from Explorer's New menu.

Allow modification of a file type

Location

> HKEY_CLASSES_ROOT\\{some file type key}

Directions

> Set the EditFlags value as specified in Table 5 to change which aspects of a file type can be modified in the File Types window (Control Panel → Folder Options → File Types tab). Note that EditFlags values can be added to combine several restrictions (01 00 00 00 + 02 00 00 00 = 03 00 00 00).

Table 5. Some of the possible EditFlags values, and what they mean

EditFlags bit	Meaning
00 00 00 00 (or omitted)	No restrictions
01 00 00 00	Not shown in the File Types window at all
02 00 00 00	Change button disabled in File Types window
08 00 00 00	Advanced button disabled in File Types window
00 01 00 00	Can't change file type description in Edit File Type window
00 02 00 00	Change Icon button disabled in Edit File Type window
40 00 00 00	Edit button disabled in Edit File Type window
80 00 00 00	Remove button disabled in Edit File Type window

Turn off the Windows Picture and Fax Viewer

Location

    HKEY_CLASSES_ROOT\SystemFileAssociations\image\
    ShellEx\ContextMenuHandlers

Directions

Delete the ShellImagePreview key to disable the Windows Picture and Fax Viewer as the default application for most image file types.

Customize the icon used for generic folders and drives

Location

    HKEY_CLASSES_ROOT\Folder\DefaultIcon

    HKEY_CLASSES_ROOT\Drive\DefaultIcon

Directions

Set the (Default) value to the full path and filename of the file containing the icon to use, followed by a comma, and then a number specifying the index of the icon to use (0 being the first icon, 1 being the second, and so on). The file you use can be an icon file (*.ico), a bitmap (*.bmp), a .dll file, an application executable (*.exe), or any other valid icon file. The default for folders is %SystemRoot%\System32\shell32.dll,3, and the default for drives is %SystemRoot%\System32\shell32.dll,8.

Add Encrypt and Decrypt commands to files' context menus

Location

    HKEY_LOCAL_MACHINE\SOFTWARE\Microsoft\Windows\
    CurrentVersion\Explorer\Advanced

Directions

Create a new DWORD value called EncryptionContextMenu, and set it to 1. Then, right-click any file (or group of files) and select Encrypt to turn on NTFS encryption for the file(s) or Decrypt to turn it off.

Customize the locations of system folders

Location

> HKEY_CURRENT_USER\Software\Microsoft\Windows\
> CurrentVersion\Explorer\Shell Folders
>
> HKEY_CURRENT_USER\Software\Microsoft\Windows\
> CurrentVersion\Explorer\User Shell Folders

Directions

> Double-click any value and type the full path of the folder you wish to be the new location of the corresponding system folder. Note that you'll have to manually move any existing files from the old location to the new one.

Open a command prompt window in any folder

Location

> HKEY_CLASSES_ROOT\Directory\shell

Directions

> Create a new key named cmd, and then set its (Default) to:
>
> > Open Command &Prompt Here
>
> Next, create a new key under cmd named command, and set its (Default) value to:
>
> > cmd.exe /k "cd %L && ver"
>
> Finally, right-click any folder and select Open Command Prompt Here to open a command prompt window rooted in the selected folder.

Performance Tweaks

These next few settings affect the performance of your system.

Turn off CD AutoPlay

Location

> HKEY_LOCAL_MACHINE\SYSTEM\CurrentControlSet\
> Services\Cdrom

Directions

Set the `Autorun` DWORD value to `0` to disable CD AutoPlay.

TIP To selectively choose how AutoPlay handles certain types of media, right-click the drive icon for your CD drive, CD recorder, or DVD drive, select Properties, and choose the AutoPlay tab.

Change the responsiveness of drop-down menus

Location

`HKEY_CURRENT_USER\Control Panel\Desktop`

Directions

Set the `MenuShowDelay` string value to the number of milliseconds (thousanths of a second) Windows will wait before opening a menu. The default is `400` (a little less than half-a-second); enter `0` (zero) here to eliminate the delay completely or a very large value (`65534` is the maximum) to disable the automatic opening of menus.

Disable programs configured to run at Windows startup

Location

`HKEY_CURRENT_USER\SOFTWARE\Microsoft\Windows\`
`CurrentVersion\Run`

`HKEY_CURRENT_USER\SOFTWARE\Microsoft\Windows\`
`CurrentVersion\RunOnce`

`HKEY_LOCAL_MACHINE\SOFTWARE\Microsoft\Windows\`
`CurrentVersion\Run`

`HKEY_LOCAL_MACHINE\SOFTWARE\Microsoft\Windows\`
`CurrentVersion\RunOnce`

Directions

Each value in these four keys represents a different program; simply delete the entry corresponding to the startup program you wish to disable. Note that values stored in the HKEY_CURRENT_USER branch are for the currently logged-in user, while entries in the HKEY_LOCAL_MACHINE apply to all users.

Choose how long Chkdsk waits before checking a drive during startup

Location
> HKEY_LOCAL_MACHINE\SYSTEM\CurrentControlSet\Control\
> Session Manager

Directions
> Set the AutoChkTimeOut DWORD value to the number of seconds Chkdsk should wait before scanning your hard disk during Windows startup.

Choose how long before Windows considers an application to be hung

Location
> HKEY_CURRENT_USER\Control Panel\Desktop

Directions
> Set the HungAppTimeout string value to the number of milliseconds (thousanths of a second) Windows will wait before it considers an application to be "Not Responding."

User Account and Network Settings

These next few settings deal with user accounts, security, logging in, and sharing resources over a network.

Disable the Unread Messages display on the Welcome screen

Location
> HKEY_CURRENT_USER\Software\Microsoft\Windows\
> CurrentVersion\UnreadMail

Directions

Set the `MessageExpiryDays` DWORD value to 0 (zero) to turn off the notification of unread messages for each user on the Welcome screen.

Hide the last logged-in username (old-style logon dialog only)

Location

`HKEY_LOCAL_MACHINE\SOFTWARE\Microsoft\Windows NT\CurrentVersion\Winlogon`

Directions

Set the `DontDisplayLastUserName` string value to 1 (one) to stop Windows from filling the username field with the last logged-in user (has no effect when used with the Welcome screen).

Customize the logon message (old-style logon dialog only)

Location

`HKEY_LOCAL_MACHINE\SOFTWARE\Microsoft\Windows NT\CurrentVersion\Winlogon`

Directions

Set the `LogonPrompt` string value to whatever text you'd like to appear at the top of the standard Windows logon dialog (has no effect when used with the Welcome screen).

Stop sharing the Scheduled Tasks folder

Location

`HKEY_LOCAL_MACHINE\SOFTWARE\Microsoft\Windows\ CurrentVersion\Explorer\RemoteComputer\NameSpace`

Directions

Delete the `{D6277990-4C6A-11CF-8D87-00AA0060F5BF}` key to stop sharing the Scheduled Tasks folder with other computers on your network, which will dramatically improve network browsing performance.

Class IDs of Interface Objects

Windows keeps track of its various components with Class IDs, 33-digit codes consisting of both letters and numbers, enclosed in {curly braces}. Class IDs are stored in the Registry under HKEY_CLASSES_ROOT\CLSID. Locate the key named for a Class ID under this branch to change any settings or behavior of the corresponding object. Use the Registry Editor's search feature to find the Class ID for an object not listed here by searching for the caption of the object.

The following is a list of the commonly used system objects and their corresponding Class IDs.

Object	Class ID
Administrative Tools	{D20EA4E1-3957-11D2-A40B-0C5020524153}
Briefcase	{85BBD920-42A0-1069-A2E4-08002B30309D}
Control Panel	{21EC2020-3AEA-1069-A2DD-08002B30309D}
Desktop	{00021400-0000-0000-C000-000000000046}
Favorites	{1A9BA3A0-143A-11CF-8350-444553540000}
Fonts	{BD84B380-8CA2-1069-AB1D-08000948F534}
Internet Explorer	{FBF23B42-E3F0-101B-8488-00AA003E56F8}
Internet Explorer ActiveX Cache	{88C6C381-2E85-11d0-94DE-444553540000}
Internet Explorer Cache	{7BD29E00-76C1-11CF-9DD0-00A0C9034933}
Internet Explorer History	{FF393560-C2A7-11CF-BFF4-444553540000}
My Computer	{20D04FE0-3AEA-1069-A2D8-08002B30309D}
My Documents	{450D8FBA-AD25-11D0-98A8-0800361B1103}
My Network Places	{208D2C60-3AEA-1069-A2D7-08002B30309D}
Network Connections	{992CFFA0-F557-101A-88EC-00DD010CCC48}
Printers and Faxes	{2227A280-3AEA-1069-A2DE-08002B30309D}
Recycle Bin	{645FF040-5081-101B-9F08-00AA002F954E}
Scanners & Cameras	{3F953603-1008-4F6E-A73A-04AAC7A992F1}
Scheduled Tasks	{D6277990-4C6A-11CF-8D87-00AA0060F5BF}
Shared Documents	{59031A47-3F72-44A7-89C5-5595FE6B30EE}

TIP   A good way to avoid having to type these codes is to do a search in the Registry. For example, if you're looking for the Recycle Bin Class ID, do a search in the Registry Editor for Recycle Bin. When it's found, make sure the code matches the one listed above (as there may be more than one), and then right-click on the key named for the code and select Rename. Right-click the highlighted text in the rename field, select Copy, and then press Esc to cancel the rename operation. The Class ID will then be placed on the clipboard, waiting to be copied to the Registry Editor's Search field or anywhere else you please.

PART VI

Command Prompt

The premise of the command prompt is simple enough: commands are typed, one at a time, at a blinking cursor, and the commands are issued when the Enter key is pressed. After a command has completed, a new prompt is shown, allowing additional commands to be typed.

To open a command prompt window, go to Start → Programs → Accessories → Command Prompt, or go to Start → Run and launch cmd.exe.

Some commands are fairly rudimentary, requiring only that you type their name. Other commands are more involved, and can require several options (sometimes called *arguments* or *command-line parameters*). For example, the del command (discussed later in this chapter) is used to delete one or more files; it requires that the name of the file be specified after the command, like this:

```
del /p myfile.txt
```

Here, *myfile.txt* is the filename to be deleted, and /p is an extra option used to modify the behavior of del. Now, the fact that this usage is not limited to internal commands (like del) is what makes the command line such an important part of Windows XP's design. For example:

```
notepad c:\folder\myfile.txt
```

is what Windows executes behind the scenes, by default, when you double-click the *myfile.txt* icon in Explorer. The Notepad application name is used as a command here; if you type the filename of any existing file at the command prompt, it instructs Windows to launch that file. This works for applications, Windows Shortcuts, batch files, documents, or any other type of file; the only requirement is that the file be located in the current working directory (see the cd command, later in this chapter) or in a folder specified in the path (also discussed later in this chapter).

> **TIP** In addition to the command prompt window, there are two other places in Windows XP that act similarly: the address bar and the Start → Run dialog. The primary difference is that neither of these interfaces recognize the internal commands listed in this chapter, nor do they remember the state from the previous command (which means that commands like cd would be meaningless).

Wildcards, Pipes, and Redirection

These symbols have special meaning when used with other commands on the command line:

Symbol	Description
*	Multiple-character wildcard, used to specify a group of files.
?	Single-character wildcard, used to specify multiple files with more precision than *.
.	One dot represents the current directory; see "cd."
..	Two dots represent the parent directory; see "cd."
\	Separates directory names, drive letters, and filenames. By itself, \ represents the root directory of the current drive.
>	Redirect a command's text output into a file instead of the console window; existing files will be overwritten.
>>	Redirect a command's text output into a file instead of the console window, appending existing files.

Symbol	Description
<	Directs the contents of a text file to a command's input; use in place of keyboard entry to automate interactive command-line applications.
|	Redirects the output of a program or command to a second program or command (this is called a "pipe").

Command Prompt Commands

Most of the following commands are not standalone applications, but rather internal functions of the Command Prompt (*cmd.exe*) application (they won't be recognized by the address bar or by Start → Run.) A few entries, such as *xcopy.exe* and *move.exe*, are actually standalone applications, but are typically useful only when called from the command prompt.

cd or chdir

With no arguments, cd displays the full pathname of the current directory. Given the pathname of an existing directory, it changes the current directory to the specified directory. The syntax is:

    cd [*directory*]

If *directory* is on a different drive (for example, if the current directory is *c:\dream* and you type cd d:\nightmare), the current working directory on *that* drive is changed, but the current working *drive* is not; that is, you'll still be in *c:\dream*. To change the current drive, simply type the letter followed by a colon, by itself, at the prompt. When you subsequently switch to the *D:* drive by typing d: at the prompt, you'll be dumped right into the *nightmare* directory.

Pathnames can be absolute (including the full path starting with the root) or relative to the current directory. A path can be optionally prefixed with a drive letter. The special paths . and .. refer to the current directory and its parent directory, respectively.

Examples

If the current drive is *C:*, to make *c:\chefs\Akira* the current directory:

```
cd \chefs\Akira
```

To change to the parent directory (here, *c:\chefs*):

```
cd ..
```

To change to the root directory of the current drive (here, *c:*):

```
cd \
```

---

cls

Type cls at the prompt to clear the screen and the screen buffer, useful for privacy concerns or simply to reduce clutter. The difference between using cls and simply closing the current command prompt window and opening a new one, is that you're working environment (such as the current directory) is preserved with cls.

cls is also useful in complex batch files, for clearing the screen after one set of interactions or command output. The name cls (Clear Screen) refers to the old days when DOS owned the whole screen.

---

copy

copy makes a complete copy of an existing file. If another file by the same name exists at *destination*, you will be asked if you want to overwrite it. Omit *destination* to copy the specified files to the current working directory. *destination* can also specify filenames, useful for renaming the files as they're being copied. copy accepts the following parameters and options:

```
copy source destination
copy [/a | /b] source [/a | /b] [+ source [/a | /b]
    [+ ...]] [destination [/a | /b]] [/v] [/y | /-y] [/d]
    [/z]
```

Option	Description
/a	Specifies that the file to copy is in ASCII format
/b	Specifies that the file to copy is a binary file

Option	Description
/v	Verifies that new files are written successfully by comparing them with the originals
/y, /-y	Suppresses or enables prompting, respectively, to confirm replacing existing files
/d	Allows the new file to be decrypted (NTFS volumes only)
/z	Copies networked files in restartable mode
+	Concatenates (glues together) several source files

Examples

```
copy c:\temp.txt d:\files\temp.txt
copy d:\cdsample\images\*.* .
copy words.txt d:\files\morewords.txt
copy *.* d:\files
```

date

If you type date on the command line without an option, the current date setting is displayed, and you are prompted for a new one. Press Enter to keep the same date. Otherwise, date accepts the following options:

```
date [/t | date]
```

Option	Description
date	Specifies the date using the mm-dd-[yy]yy format. Separate month, day, and year with periods, hyphens, or slashes.
/t	Displays the current date without prompting for a new one.

del or erase

The del command is used to delete one or more files from the command line *without* sending them to the Recycle Bin. The del options are:

```
del [/p] [/f] [/s] [/q] [/a:attributes] filename
```

Option	Description
filename	Specifies the file(s) to delete (* and ? wildcards are supported)
/p	Prompts for confirmation before deleting each file
/f	Forces deleting of read-only files
/s	Deletes specified files in all subdirectories (when using wildcards)
/q	Quiet mode; do not prompt if filename is *.*
/a:attributes	Selects files to delete based on attributes (read-only, hidden, system, or archive)

Examples

```
del myfile.txt
del c:\files\myfile.txt
del c:\files\myfile.* /p
```

dir

Without any options, dir displays the disk's volume label and serial number, a list of all files and subdirectories in the current directory, file/directory size, date/time of last modification, long filename, the total number of files listed, their cumulative size, and the free space (in bytes) remaining on the disk. If you specify one or more file or directory names (* and ? wildcards are supported), information only for those files or directories will be listed. dir accepts the following options:

```
dir [filename] [/b] [/c] [/d] [/l] [/n] [/p] [/q] [/s]
    [/w] [/x] [/4] [/a:attributes] [/o:sortorder]
    [/t:timefield]
```

Option	Description
/a:attributes	Display only files with/without specified attributes (using – as a prefix specifies "not," and a colon between the option and attribute is optional).
/b	Use bare format (no heading information or summary). Use with /s to find a filename.
/c	Display compression ratio of files on Dblspace or DrvSpace drives, assuming 16 sectors per cluster.

Option	Description
/d	Same as /w, except files are sorted vertically.
/l	Use lowercase.
/n	List files in a "new" Unix-like display, where filenames are shown on the right.
/o:*sortorder*	List files in sorted order (using – as a prefix reverses the order, and a colon between the option and attribute is optional): d = date and time (earliest first), e = alphabetically by extension, g = group directories first , n = alphabetically by name, s = size (smallest first).
/p	Pause after each screenful of information; press any key to continue.
/q	Display the owner of each file.
/s	Include all files in all subdirectories, in addition to those in the current directory.
/t:*timefield*	Controls which time is used when sorting: c = created, a = last accessed, w = last modified (written)
/w	Wide list format. File and directory names are listed in five columns, and are sorted horizontally. Use /d instead to sort vertically.
/x	Include the "short" 8.3 versions of long filenames. For example, *Sam's File.txt* has an alternate filename, *samsfi~1.txt* to maintain compatibilty with older applications.
/4	Display the listed years as four digits. By default, two-digit years are displayed.

Examples

```
dir
dir *.txt
dir \ /s /os > allfiles.txt
dir \\bubba\cdrom
```

echo

echo is typically used with other commands or in a batch file to display text on the screen. The following options can be used with echo:

```
echo [on | off | message]
```

Option	Description
on | off	Turns on or off command echoing in batch files. To turn echoing off without displaying the echo off command itself, type @echo off.
message	Types the message you'd like displayed to the screen.

exit

Typing exit has the same effect as closing the command prompt window with the [x] button. exit accepts the following options:

    exit [/b] [*exitcode*]

Option	Description
/b	If exit is used from within a batch file, it will close the current command prompt window. Specify /b to simply exit the batch file but leave *cmd.exe* running.
exitcode	Specifies a numerical "exit code" number that is passed to the application or process that launched the command prompt or started the batch file.

find

\Windows\Command\find.exe

After searching the specified files, find displays any lines of text that contain the string you've specified for your search. find is useful for searching for specific words (strings) in files, but don't get it confused with Start → Search → For Files or Folders, which is capable of searching for text, files, directories, etc., and has many other capabilities that the find command doesn't have. The find options are:

    find [/v] [/c] [/n] [/i] [/offline] "*string*"
        [*filename*[...]]

Option	Description
"*string*"	The text to look for, enclosed in quotation marks.
filename	The file(s) in which to search. Although wildcards (*, ?) are not supported, multiple filenames can be specified as long as they are separated with commas. If filename is omitted, find searches text typed at the prompt or piped from another command via the pipe character (|).
/c	Displays only the count of lines containing the string.

Option	Description
/i	Ignores the case of characters when searching for the string.
/n	Displays line numbers with the displayed lines.
/v	Displays all lines not containing the specified string.
/offline	Include files with the offline attribute set (that otherwise would be skipped).

Examples

```
find "redflag" myexployees.txt
find /c "deceased" myexployees.txt
for %f in (*.bat) do find "cls" %f >> cls.txt
```

for

Use this command to repeat a specified command any number of times. You specify an arbitrary variable name and a set of values to be iterated through. For each value in the set, the command is repeated. The options used by for are the following:

```
for [/d] %variable in (set) do command [arguments]
for /r [path] %variable in (set) do command [arguments]
for /l %variable in (start,step,end) do command
    [arguments]
```

Option	Description
command [arguments]	The command to execute or the program filename to run.
%variable	A one-letter variable name that is assigned, one-by-one, to the elements listed in set. When used in a batch file, the variable name must be preceded by two percent signs.
set	The sequence of elements through which the for command cycles. Elements are separated with spaces, and can be files, strings, or numbers. Use the /l option for the more traditional start,step,end format.
/d	Instructs for to match against directory names instead of filenames if set contains wildcards. Can't be used with the /l or /r options.
/l	Specifies that set takes the form of start,step,end, allowing you to specify a range of numbers and an increment instead of having to list each element.

Option	Description
/r [path]	Recursively executes command for each directory and subdirectory in path. If path is omitted, the current directory is used. Without /r, files specified in set only relate to the current directory. If set is just a single period (.), for will simply list all the directories in the tree.

Examples

Loop three times, assigning words to the variable %n:

```
for %n in (rock paper scissors) do echo %n
```

Both of the following loops are equivalent. They repeat five times, assigning numbers 1, 2, 3, 4, and 5 to the variable %n:

```
for %n in (1 2 3 4 5) do md ch%n
for /l %n in (1,1,5) do md ch%n
```

More examples:

```
for /l %n in (100,-2,0) do echo %n
for %j in (a.txt b.txt c.txt) do copy %j a:
for %x in (*.txt) do type %x
for /r c:\ %i in (.) do echo %i
```

md or mkdir

Use md to make a directory (folder), rooted in the current directory (set with cd). The syntax is:

```
md [drive:]path
```

Examples

```
md harry
md c:\olddir\newdir
```

Note that folder names with spaces must be enclosed in quotation marks; the following two commands yield different results:

```
C:\>md rolling stones
C:\>md "rolling stones"
```

more   \windows\system32\more.com

more displays one screen of text at a time. More is often used as a filter with other commands that may send a lot of output to the

---

screen (i.e., to read standard input from a pipe or redirected file). Press any key to see the next screenful of output. Press Ctrl-C to end the output before it is done. more accepts the following options:

```
more /e [/c] [/p] [/s] [/tn] [+n] [filename]
more [/e [/c] [/p] [/s] [/tn] [+n]] < filename
   {some other command} | more [/e [/c] [/p] [/s] [/tn]
   [+n]]
```

Option	Description
filename	Specifies the name of a file to display.
/c	Clears the screen before displaying file.
/e	If the /e option is specified, the following additional extended commands are available at the -- More -- prompt: P*n*: display next *n* lines, S*n*: skip next *n* lines, Spacebar: display next page, Enter: display next line, F: display next file, Q: quit, =: show line number, ?: show help.
/p	Expands form-feed characters.
/s	Squeezes multiple blank lines into a single line.
/t*n*	Expands tabs characters to *n* spaces (default 8).
/+*n*	Starts display of the file at line *n*.

Examples

```
C:\>more c:\windows\readme.txt
C:\>type c:\windows\readme.txt | more
C:\>dir c:\windows | more
```

---

move   \windows\system32\move.exe

move works like copy, except that the source is deleted after the copy is complete. *Filename* can be a single file, a group of files (separated with commas), or a single file specification with wildcards. The move options are:

```
move [/y | /-y] filename[,...] destination
```

Option	Description
filename	Specifies the location and name(s) of the file or files you want to move. Wildcards (*, ?) are supported.
destination	Specifies the new location (and optionally, the new name) of the file. The destination parameter can consist of a drive, a directory name, or a combination of the two.

Option	Description
/y, /-y	Suppresses or enables prompting, respectively, to confirm the creation of a directory or overwriting of the destination.

Examples

```
C:\>move myfile.txt d:\files\
C:\>move myfile.txt d:\files\newfile.txt
C:\>move d:\files myfiles
```

path

When you type an executable filename at the command prompt (as opposed to an internal DOS command), Windows starts by looking in the current directory for a file that matches. If no matching file is found, Windows then looks in a series of other folders—these folders are known collectively as the *path*, or the command search path. The path statement is used to define these additional directories, and is used as follows:

```
path [path1][;path2][;path3][;...]
```

Examples

```
C:\>path c:\stuff;d:\tools
C:\>path %path%;c:\stuff;d:\tools
```

prompt

Change the appearance of the prompt. Type prompt by itself (without *text*) to reset the prompt to its default setting, or use this syntax:

```
prompt [text]
```

Text can contain normal characters and the following special codes:

Char	Description	Char	Description
$_	Carriage return and linefeed	$h	Erase previous character
$$	$ (dollar sign)	$l	< (less-than sign)
$a	& (ampersand)	$n	Current drive
$b	| (pipe)	$p	Current drive and path

Char	Description	Char	Description
$c	((left parenthesis)	$q	= (equal sign)
$d	Current date	$s	(single space)
$e	Escape character, for formatting	$t	Current time
$f	) (right parenthesis)	$v	Windows version number
$g	> (greater-than sign), karet		

Examples

```
prompt $p$g
prompt $p$_$d$g
prompt $n$g
```

rd or rmdir

rd is used to delete empty directories, and optionally, to delete directories and their contents. Unlike in Windows Explorer, files and folders are deleted differently; if you try to use del to delete a directory, it will simply delete all the files in the directory, but the directory itself will remain. rd accepts the following options:

```
rd [/s] [/q] path
```

Option	Description
path	Specifies the directory to delete.
/s	Removes all files and subdirectories of the specified directory.
/q	Quiet mode; don't prompt when using /s.

ren or rename

Use ren to rename any single file or directory, or even several files at once via wildcards, * and ?. The syntax is:

```
ren [filename1] [filename2]
```

where *filename1* is the name of the existing object, and *filename2* is the new name to assign.

Examples

```
rename myfile.txt file.txt
ren "chap 5.doc" "sect 5.doc"
ren chap?5.doc sect?5.doc
ren chap*.doc revchap*.doc
ren *.htm *.html
```

---

set

The set command manipulates environment variables from the command line.

 TIP Because the command prompt's environment is reset when its window is closed, the usefulness of set is fairly limited. To affect more permanent changes to environment variables, go to Control Panel → System → Advanced tab → Environment variables.

Type set without options to display all the current environment variables, or use this syntax:

```
set [variable[=[string]]]
set /p variable=[promptstring]
set /a expression
```

Type set with only a variable name (no equal sign or value) to display a list of all the variables whose prefix matches the name. The set options are:

Option	Description
variable	Specifies the variable name. If variable is specified by itself, its value is displayed. If variable is specified by itself with an equals sign, the variable is assigned an empty value and deleted. variable cannot contain spaces.
string	Specifies a series of characters to assign to variable. This can contain references to other variables by surrounding them with preceding and trailing percent signs (%).
/p	Specifies that variable will be assigned by text input from the user, rather than string.
promptstring	The text prompt to display when using the /p option.

Option	Description
/a	Specifies that expression is a numerical expression to be evaluated.
expression	When used with the /a option, expression is a collection of symbols, numbers, and variables arranged so that it can be evaluated by set. The following symbols are recognized (in decreasing order of precedence): ( ) ! ~ */ +- << >> & ^ | = *= /= %= += -= &= ^= |= <<= >>=

Examples

```
C:\>set dummy=not much
C:\>set dircmd=/s /o-s
C:\>set path=%path%;c:\mystuff
C:\>set prompt=$t>
C:\>set /p dummy=Enter text here>
C:\>set /a 7+(3*4)
```

You can reference environment variables with other commands:

```
C:\>set workdir=C:\stuff\tim's draft
C:\>cd %workdir%
```

Table 6 shows most of Windows' predefined variables.

Table 6. Predefined Windows variables

Variable	Description
ALLUSERSPROFILE	The location of the *All Users* folder, usually *c:\Documents and Settings\All Users*.
APPDATA	The location of the Application Data folder, usually *c:\Documents and Settings\%USERNAME%\Application Data*.
COMMONPROGRAMFILES	The location of the Common Files folder, usually *c:\Program Files\Common Files*.
COMPUTERNAME	The network name of the computer, set by going to Control Panel → System → Computer Name tab → Change.
COMSPEC	The location of the command prompt application executable, *c:\Windows\system32\cmd.exe* by default.
COPYCMD	Whether the copy, move, and xcopy commands should prompt for confirmation before overwriting a file. The default value is /-y. To stop the warning messages, set COPYCMD to /y.

Table 6. Predefined Windows variables (continued)

Variable	Description
DIRCMD	Specifies the default options for the dir command. For example, setting DIRCMD to /p will cause dir to always pause after displaying a screenful of output.
HOMEDRIVE	The drive letter of the drive containing the current user's home directory, usually *c:*, used with HOMEPATH.
HOMEPATH	Along with HOMEDRIVE, the path of the current user's home directory, usually *\Documents and Settings\ %USERNAME%*.
LOGONSERVER	The name of the computer as seen by other computers on your network, usually the same as COMPUTERNAME preceded by two backslashes.
OS	Used to identify the operating system to some applications; for Windows XP, OS is set to "Windows_NT." You may be able to "fool" an older program that is programmed not to run on an NT system by changing this variable temporarily.
PATH	The sequence of directories in which the command interpreter will look for commands to be interpreted. See "path," earlier in this chapter.
PATHEXT	The filename extensions (file types) Windows will look for in the directories listed in the path (see "path," earlier in this chapter). The default is .COM;.EXE;.BAT;.CMD;.VBS;. VBE;.JS;.JSE;.WSF;.WSH.
PROGRAMFILES	The location of the *Program Files* folder, usually *c:\Program Files*.
PROMPT	The format of the command-line prompt, usually PG. See "prompt," earlier in this chapter, for details.
SESSIONNAME	The name of the current command prompt session; usually "Console."
SYSTEMDRIVE	The drive letter of the drive containing Windows, usually *c:*.
SYSTEMROOT	The location of the *Windows* directory (or more specifically, the name of the folder in which the *\Windows\ System32* folder can be found), usually *c:\windows*.
TEMP and TMP	The location where many programs will store temporary files. TEMP and TMP are two different variables, but they should both have the same value. Usually set to *C:\ DOCUME~1\%USERNAME%\LOCALS~1\Temp* (short name used to maintain compatibility with older DOS programs).

Table 6. Predefined Windows variables (continued)

Variable	Description
USERDOMAIN	The name of the domain to which the computer belongs (set by going to Control Panel → System → Computer Name → Change). If no domain is specified, USERDOMAIN is the same as COMPUTERNAME.
USERNAME	The name of the current user.
USERPROFILE	The location of the current user's home directory, which should be the same as HOMEDRIVE plus HOMEPATH, usually *c:\Documents and Settings\%USERNAME%*.
WINDIR	The location of the Windows directory, usually *c:\windows*.

sort
\windows\system32\sort.exe

The sort command sorts text on a line-by-line basis. sort is often used in conjunction with either pipes or output redirection (see the beginning of this chapter), wherein you can sort the output of another command. sort takes the following options:

```
sort [/r] [/+n] [/m kilobytes] [/rec recordbytes]
    [/t [tempdir]] [/o outputfilename] [filename]
```

Option	Description
/r	Reverses the sort order; that is, sorts Z to A, then 9 to 0.
/+n	Sorts the file according to characters in column *n*.
/m kilobytes	Specifies amount of main memory to allocate for the sort operation, in kilobytes (160 kb being the minimum).
/rec recordbytes	Specifies the maximum number of characters on a line (in a record); the default is 4096, and the maximum is 65,535.
/t tempdir	Specifies the location of the folder used to store temporary files in case the data does not fit in main memory (see /m).
/o outputfilename	Specifies a file where the output is to be stored. If not specified, the sorted data is displayed at the prompt. Using the /o option is faster than redirecting output (with the > symbol).
filename	The name (and optionally, full path) of the file to sort.

Examples

```
dir | sort
sort /o results.txt data.txt
sort data.txt > results.txt
type data.txt | sort > results.txt
```

time

If you type time on the command line without an option, the current time setting is displayed, and you are prompted for a new one. Press Enter to keep the same date. The time options are:

```
time [/t | time]
```

Option	Description
time	Sets the system time using the format hh:mm:ss [A|P].
/t	Displays the current time without prompting for a new one.

type

The type command is used to quickly view the contents of any text file (especially short files). type is also useful for concatenating text files, using the >> operator.

Examples

```
type c:\boot.ini
type c:\stuff\readme.txt | more
type a.txt b.txt >> c.txt
```

ver

ver shows the version of Windows you're using. You can also find the Windows version at Control Panel → System → General tab, but it won't show you the revision number.

xcopy   *\windows\system32\xcopy.exe*

xcopy works like copy, but provides more options, works with multiple directories, and is often faster. The xcopy32 options are:

```
xcopy source [destination] [/a | /m] [/d[:date]] [/p]
    [/s [/e]] [/v] [/w] [/c] [/i] [/q] [/f] [/l] [/g] [/h]
    [/r] [/t] [/u] [/k] [/n] [/o] [/x] [/y] [/-y] [/z]
    [/exclude:filenames]
```

Option	Description
source	Specifies the file(s) to copy; source must include the full path.
destination	Specifies the location and/or names of new files. If omitted, files are copied to the current directory.
/a	Copies files with the archive attribute set, but doesn't change the attribute of the source file (similar to /m).
/c	Continues copying even if errors occur.
/d:date	Copies only files changed on or after the specified date. If no date is given, copies only those source files that are newer than existing destination files.
/e	Copies all directories and subdirectories (everything), including empty ones (similar to /s). May be used to modify /t.
/exclude:filenames	Specifies a file (or a list of files) containing strings of text (each on its own line). When any of the strings match any part of the absolute path of the file to be copied, that file will be excluded from being copied. Contrary to what you might expect, filenames does not actually list the filenames to exclude.
/f	Displays full paths while copying (unless /q is specified); normally, only filenames are displayed.
/h	Allows the copying of encrypted files to destination that does not support encryption; otherwise, such files are skipped.
/h	Copies hidden and system files also; normally files with the hidden or system attributes are skipped.
/i	If a destination is not supplied and you are copying more than one file, assumes that the destination must be a directory. (By default, xcopy asks if the destination is a file or directory.)
/k	Duplicates the attributes of the source files; by default, xcopy turns off the read-only attributes.
/l	Displays files that would be copied given other options, but does not actually copy the files.
/m	Copies files with the archive attribute set, then turns off the archive attribute of the source file (similar to /a).
/n	Copies files using short (8.3) file and directory names (for example, PROGRA~1 instead of Program Files). Use this feature to convert an entire branch of files and folders to their short names.

Option	Description
/o	Copies file ownership and ACL information.
/p	Prompts you before creating each destination file.
/q	Quiet mode; does not display filenames while copying.
/r	Overwrites read-only files.
/s	Copies directories and subdirectories, except empty ones (similar to /e).
/t	Creates the directory structure, but does not copy files; does not include empty directories unless /e is specified.
/u	Copies from the source only files that already exist on destination; used to update files.
/v	Verifies copied files by comparing them to the originals.
/w	Prompts you to press a key before copying (useful in batch files).
/x	Copies file audit settings (implies /o).
/y, /-y	Suppress or enable prompting, respectively, to confirm replacing existing files.
/z	Copies networked files in restartable mode.

Examples

Copy all the files and subdirectories, including any empty subdirectories and hidden files, from *c:\foobar* to the root directory of *d:*

```
C:\>xcopy \foobar d: /s /e /h
```

Windows Recovery Console

The Windows Recovery Console (WRC) is a tool included with Windows XP, used to repair the operating system when it won't start, as well as perform some other tasks not otherwise possible from within Windows. For those accustomed to being able to boot into DOS to effect repairs in some earlier versions of Windows, the WRC is the Windows XP equivalent.

The WRC allows you to do the following:

- Repair a Windows XP installation, including the filesystem boot sector, the Master Boot Record (MBR), and the Boot Manager configuration

- Copy, rename, delete, or replace operating system files that otherwise cannot be modified while Windows is running

- Enable or disable services or devices

- Create and format hard drive partitions

To get into the WRC, you'll need to boot up off the Windows XP CD. After Setup loads all its drivers, press R to start the Windows Recovery Console.

You can also install the Recovery Console to your hard disk so that it can be started without the CD. This option, which will add it to the Boot Manager menu, is useful if you find that you need the Recovery Console frequently or you're unable to boot off the CD. To install the WRC, insert your Windows CD, go to Start → Run, and type *d:*\i386\winnt32. exe /cmdcons, where *d:* is the drive letter of your CD drive.

Regardless of how the WRC is started, you'll be greeted with a rather unfriendly warning message, followed by the following prompt:

```
Which Windows installation would you like to logon to
(enter to abort)?
```

Choose whatever number corresponds to the Windows installation you wish to repair (usually 1), and log in using your Administrator password. If you've forgotten your Administrator password (set when Windows XP was installed), WRC won't let you in. You'll have three tries before WRC reboots your system. If this is the case, and Windows won't start, you may have to reinstall Windows XP.

Once you've logged in, the WRC looks and feels like the Windows XP command prompt described at the beginning of this chapter, but it's not exactly the same. You can execute most of the standard DOS commands (albeit in a more limited fashion), but you won't be able to launch DOS or Windows programs.

Recovery Console Commands

The following DOS commands, documented earlier in this chapter, can be used in the Windows Recovery Console: attrib, cd, cls, copy, del, dir, exit, md, more, ren, rd, set, and type. In addition, you'll be able to use the Chkdsk, DiskPart, and Format utilities discussed in Part III. The following are the special commands that are available in the Windows Recovery Console:

Command	Description
batch filename [outputfile]	Executes a batch file, something that can't be accomplished in the WRC by typing the filename alone, as in the real command prompt.

bootcfg / command	Starts the Boot Manager configuration and recovery tool. This tool is used to view, edit, and rebuild the *boot.ini* file, which contains a list of all installed operating systems on a multiple-boot system. Command can be any of the following:
	 add
	     Adds a new entry to the boot.ini file.
	 copy
	     Creates a backup of the boot.ini configuration file.
	 default
	     Sets the default boot entry.
	 disableredirect
	     Disables redirection instigated by the redirect command.
	 list
	     Displays the entries currently specified in *boot.ini*.
	 rebuild
	     Lists all the Windows installations and selectively rebuilds the boot menu. Tip: Use bootcfg /copy before using rebuild.
	 redirect [port baudrate | useBiosSettings]
	     Enables redirection of the boot loader output to the specified serial port and baudrate, or use useBiosSettings to use the default COM port settings in the system BIOS.
	 scan
	     Scans your hard disk for all Windows installations and displays a list of the results, independent of the contents of *boot.ini*.

Command	Description
disable [service | device_driver]	Disables a system service or a device driver for the next time Windows starts. See enable, below, for details.
enable service | device_driver [startup_type]	Starts or enables a system service or a device driver for the next time Windows starts. Use the listsvc command to list the names of all available services and device drivers. The startup_type option can be SERVICE_BOOT_START, SERVICE_SYSTEM_START, SERVICE_AUTO_START, or SERVICE_DEMAND_START.
fixboot [drive]	Writes a new partition boot sector onto the specified drive letter. In most cases, you can omit drive to use the current partition. Use this command to fix the partition boot sector if it has been damaged, typically by a virus or the installation of another operating system.
fixmbr [device]	Repairs the master boot record of the specified disk. Use the map command to display the entries for device. In most cases, you can omit device to use the default boot device, upon which your primary operating system is installed. Use this if the boot record has been damaged, typically by a virus or the installation of another operating system.
listsvc	Lists the services and drivers available on the computer, for use with the enable and disable commands discussed above.
logon	Logs on to another Windows XP/2000 installation (assuming you have more than one) without having to reboot and reenter the Recovery Console.
map	Displays drive letter mappings for use with the fixmbr command.
systemroot	Changes the current directory (like the cd command) to the "systemroot" directory (usually *c:\windows*).

Lifting Recovery Console Restrictions

By default, the attrib, copy, del, dir, and ren commands don't support wildcards (* and ?) in the Windows Recovery Console. While this is a safety feature intended to prevent unintentional damage to the system, it can be a frustrating limitation. To lift this restriction, type:

```
set AllowWildcards = true
```

TIP When typing any of the set commands, you must include spaces before and after each of the equals signs. Otherwise, you'll receive a "syntax error" message.

Another restriction is one placed on the `cd` command, wherein your access is restricted to certain directories unless you type:

```
set AllowAllPaths = true
```

To enable access to the floppy drive, type:

```
set AllowRemovableMedia = true
```

Finally, to turn off the prompt that appears when you try to replace a file with the copy command, type

```
set NoCopyPrompt = true
```

Unfortunately, these are only temporary settings and are lost as soon as the system is restarted.

WARNING

You may encounter an error in which the set command is currently disabled; unfortunately, this can only be fixed by returning to Windows and following this procedure: Start the Local Security Settings editor (*secpol.msc*) and navigate to \Security Settings\Local Policies\Security Options in the tree. Double-click the "Recovery Console: Allow floppy copy and access to all drives and all folders" entry, select Enabled → OK.

PART VII

Security Checklist

Security is a very real concern for any computer connected to a network or the Internet. There are three main categories of security threats:

A deliberate, targetted attack through your network connection
Ironically, this is the type of attack most people fear, but realistically, it is the least likely to occur, at least where home and small office networks are concerned. It's possible for a so-called hacker to obtain access to your computer, either through your Internet connection or from another computer on your local network; just not terribly likely that such a hacker will bother.

An automated invasion by a virus, robot, or Trojan horse
A *virus* is a computer program that is designed to duplicate itself with the purpose of infecting as many computers as possible. If your networked computer is infected by a virus, it might use your network connection to infect other computers; likewise, if another computer on your network is infected, your computer is vulnerable to infection. The same goes for Internet connections, although the method of transport is typically an infected email attachment.

There also exist so-called *robots*, programs that are designed to scan large groups of IP addresses, looking for vulnerabilities. The motive for such a program can be anything from exploitation of credit card numbers or other sensitive information to the hijacking of computers for the purpose of distributing spam, viruses, or extreme right-wing propoganda.

Finally, a *Trojan horse* is a program that works somewhat like a virus, except that its specific purpose is to create vulnerabilities in your computer that can subsequently be exploited by a hacker or robot. For example, a program might open a port on your computer and then communicate with a remote system to announce its presence.

A deliberate attack by a person sitting at your computer

A person who sits down at your computer can easily gain access to sensitive information, including your documents, email, and even various passwords stored by your web browser. An intruder can be anyone, from the person who steals your computer to a co-worker casually walking by your unattended desk. Naturally, it's up to you to determine the actual likelihood of such a threat, and to take the appropriate measures, such as requiring that a password be typed to get out of the screensaver.

Closing Back Doors in Windows XP

Windows XP includes several features that will enable you to implement a reasonable level of security without purchasing additional software or hardware. Unfortunately, Windows is not configured for optimal security by default. The following steps will help you close some of these back doors:

1. By default, the file sharing service is enabled for Internet connections, but in most cases, there's no reason for this. Open the Network Connections window, right-click the icon corresponding to your Internet connection, and select Properties. In the General tab, clear the checkbox next to the "File and Printer Sharing for Microsoft Networks" option. If you have more than one Internet connection icon, repeat this for each of the others, but leave it enabled for the connection to your workgroup (if applicable).

2. One of the main reasons to set up a workgroup is to share files and printers with other computers. But it's wise to share only those folders that need to be shared,

and disable sharing for all others. A feature called Simple File Sharing, which could allow anyone, anywhere, to access your personal files without your knowledge, is turned on by default in Windows XP. Go to Control Panel → Folder Options → View tab, and turn *off* the "Use simple file sharing" option.

3. Another feature, called Universal Plug & Play (UPnP), can open additional vulnerabilities on your system. UPnP is a collection of standards that allow such devices to announce their presence to UPnP servers on your network, similarly to how your PnP sound card announces its presence to Windows when you boot your system.

    Windows XP supports UPnP out of the box, but UPnP is a service that most users don't need. Unless you specifically need to connect to a UPnP device on your network, you should disable UPnP on your system *immediately* or risk exposing your system to several security threats.

    To disable UPnP, open the Services window (*services.msc*). Find the SSDP Discovery Service in the list and double-click it. Click Stop to stop the service and change the Startup type to Disabled to prevent it from loading the next time Windows starts. Click OK and then do the same for the Universal Plug and Play Device Host.

4. The Remote Desktop feature is enabled by default in Windows XP. Unless you specifically need this feature, it should be disabled. Go to Control Panel → System → Remote tab, and turn off both of the options in this window.

5. Make sure each and every user account on your system has a unique password. Even though you may not be concerned about security between users, unprotected accounts can be exploited by an attack over a network.

6. Use the Internet Connection Firewall (ICF) feature, or, better yet, obtain a router with a built-in firewall, to further protect your computer by strictly controlling network traffic into and out of your computer.

Open the Network Connections window, right-click the connection icon corresponding to your Internet connection, and select Properties. In most cases, it will be the Ethernet adapter connected to your Internet connection device. (If you're using a DSL or cable connection that requires a login with a username or password, the icon to use is the Broadband connection icon corresponding to your PPPoE connection.) Choose the Advanced tab, and turn on the "Protect my computer and network by limiting or preventing access to this computer from the Internet" option.

> **TIP**   If you find that some things stop working after enabling the firewall, return to the Advanced tab of the Properties dialog, and click Settings. Each checked entry represents a port through which communication is *allowed*. Click Add to add a new rule, and specify 127.0.0.1 for the Name or IP address. See the next section for details on which port number correspond to which services; for example, specify port 123 to get the Internet Time feature to work while the ICF is enabled.

7. The messenger service (different than Windows Messenger) allows users to send text messages to others on their local network. Unfortunately, this feature is sometimes exploited by spammers who use a command like net send * Hello World, which results in a pop-up window to appear on the Desktops of all computers in the subnet. To disable this, open the Services window (*services.msc*), and double-click the Messenger entry in the list. Click Stop to close the service, and then select Disabled from the Startup type list to prevent it from loading automatically the next time Windows starts.

8. Finally, look for vulnerabilities in your system by scanning for open ports, as described in the next section.

Scan Your System for Open Ports

Each open network port on your computer is a potential security vulnerability. Fortunately, there's a way to scan your computer for open ports so you know which holes to patch. Start by opening a command prompt window (*cmd.exe*) and running utility by typing netstat /a /o. The Active Connections utility displays its information in these five columns:

Column	Description
Proto	This will be either TCP or UDP, representing the protocol being used.
Local Address	This column has two components: the computer name and either a port number or the name of a service.
Foreign Address	For active connections, you'll see the name or IP address of the remote machine, followed by the port number. For inactive connections (showing only the open ports), you'll typically see only *:*.
State	This shows the state of the connection (TCP ports only). For server processes, you'll usually see LISTENING here, signifying that the process has opened the port and is waiting for an incoming connection. For connections originating from your computer, such as a web browser downloading a page or an active Telnet session, you'll see ESTABLISHED here.
PID	This is the Process Identifier of the application or service that is responsible for opening the port; see the rest of this section for help with matching up the PID with an application or process.

WARNING

Don't be alarmed if you see a lot of open ports. Just make sure you thoroughly track down each one, making sure it doesn't pose a security threat.

Matching a PID with a Program

Netstat shows the PID of running programs that have opened ports, but not the application names. To find out more, open Task Manager (launch *taskmgr.exe* or right-click an empty area of your taskbar and select Task Manager), and choose the Processes tab. If you don't see a column labelled PID, go to View → Select Columns, turn on the PID (Process Identifier) option, and click OK. Finally, turn on the Show processes from all users option at the bottom of the Windows Task Manager window. You can then sort the listing by PID by clicking the PID column header. The program filename is shown in the Image Name column.

NOTE

You may see *svchost.exe* listed in the Windows Task Manager, and reported by the Active Connections utility as being responsible for one or more open ports. This program is merely used to start the services listed in the Services window (*Services.msc*).

Common TCP/IP Ports

When your web browser or email program connects to another computer on the Internet, it does so through a TCP/IP port. If you have a web server or FTP server running on your computer, it opens a port to which other computers can connect. Port numbers are used to distinguish one network service from another.

A firewall uses ports (listed in the following table) to form its rules about which types of network traffic to allow, and which to prohibit. And the Active Connections utility, described previously, allows you to uncover vulnerabilities in your system using ports.

NOTE

Some firewalls make a distinction between TCP (Transmission Control Protocol) and UDP (User Datagram Protocol) ports, which is typically unecessary. In most cases, programs that use the more common TCP protocol will use the same port numbers as their counterparts that use the less-reliable UDP protocol.

Port	Description
21	FTP (File Transfer Protocol)
22	SSH (Secure Shell)
23	Telnet
25	SMTP (Simple Mail Transfer Protocol), used for sending email
43	WhoIs
53	DNS (Domain Name Server), used for looking up domain names
79	Finger
80	HTTP (Hyper Text Transfer Protocol), used by web browsers to download standard web pages
110	POP3 (Post Office Protocol, Version 3), used for retreiving email
119	NNTP (Network News Transfer Protocol), used for newsgroups
123	NTP (Network Time Protocol), used for XP's Internet Time feature
143	IMAP4 (Internet Mail Access Protocol Version 4)
220	IMAP3 (Internet Mail Access Protocol Version 3)
443	HTTPS (HTTP over TLS/SSL), used by web browsers to download secure web pages
445	File sharing for Microsoft Windows networks
563	NNTPS (Network News Transfer Protocol over SSL), used for secure newsgroups
1701	VPN (Virtual Private Networking) over L2TP
1723	VPN (Virtual Private Networking) over PPTP
3389	Remote Desktop Sharing (Microsoft Terminal Services)
580x 590x	VNC (Virtual Network Computing)
6699	Peer-to-peer file sharing, used by Napster-like programs

Other Titles Available from O'Reilly

Microsoft Windows

Windows XP in a Nutshell

*By David A. Karp, Tim O'Reilly &
Troy Mott*
1st Edition April 2002
640 pages, ISBN 0-596-00249-1

Here is a book for the power user
who is familiar with a previous version of Microsoft Windows and
wants to go deeper into the system
than the average Windows user does.
Rather than a beginner's guide or
tutorial, this straightforward reference delivers more than 500 pages of
concentrated information. For those
who are ready to customize the system or take on daily troubleshoot-
ing, *Windows XP in a Nutshell* will
unlock the hidden power of Windows XP.

Windows XP Annoyances

By David A. Karp
1st Edition October 2002
586 pages, ISBN 0-596-00416-8

This book is not here to complain or
to criticize. Rather, the mission of
Windows XP Annoyances is to
acknowledge the problems and
shortcomings of the latest Windows
operating system-and the software
that runs on it-in an effort to overcome them. Complete with a collection of tools and techniques, this
book allows users to improve their
experience with Windows XP and
establish control of the machine-
rather than the other way around.

Windows XP The Home Edition: The Missing Manual

By David Pogue
1st Edition May 2002
584 pages, ISBN 0-596-00260-2

Our latest from the Missing Manual
series begins with a tour of the
Desktop and the new two-column
Start menu, and tips for customizing
the Taskbar and toolbars. Later chapters explore each control panel and
built-in application, walk through
every conceivable configuration, and
show how to set up a small network
and share a single Internet connection among several PCs. Finally, special chapters celebrate the standard
rituals of Windows life: trou-
bleshooting, installation, and
upgrading.

Windows XP Pro: The Missing Manual

*By Craig Zacker, Linda Zacker &
David Pogue*
1st Edition January 2003
672 pages, ISBN 0-596-00348-X

Windows XP is the latest, most reli-
able, and best-looking version of the
world's most widely used operating
system, combining the extremely sta-
ble engine of Windows 2000 with
the far superior compatibility of
Windows Me. But one major failing
of Windows remains unaddressed in
the XP edition: It comes without a
single page of printed instructions.

Windows Me: The Missing Manual

By David Pogue
1st Edition September 2000
423 pages, ISBN 0-596-00009-X

In *Windows Me: The Missing Manual*, author David Pogue provides the friendly, authoritative book that should have been in the box. It's the ideal user's guide for the world's most popular operating system.

Windows Me Annoyances

By David A. Karp
1st Edition March 2001
472 pages, ISBN 0-596-00060-X

Based on the author's popular *Annoyances.org* web sites, *Windows Me Annoyances* is an authoritative collection of techniques for customizing Windows Me. Packed with creative and seldom-documented ways to quickly identify and fix a particular annoyance or customize Windows for individual needs, it's the definitive resource for dealing with crashes, unintelligible error messages, unwanted icons, and much more.